C000214529

"At times painful, but also p
shines a light on what p
Britain. Barnard encour
future, and rightly sugges... ...... ,

TORSTEN BELL, Resolution Foundation

"A clear, perceptive and timely discussion of poverty in the UK that for
all its authority never loses sight of a key question: how did we, as a
society that prides itself on being compassionate and just, get *here*?"

PATRICK BUTLER, Social Policy Editor, *The Guardian*

"Helen Barnard distills all her extensive expertise on modern
poverty into this book – the result is a vital primer for
anyone thinking of having an opinion on this subject."

BEN CHU, Economics Editor, *Newsnight*

"Helen Barnard is consistently one of the most interesting
thinkers on social policy in Britain, even when – or
perhaps especially when – you disagree with her."

ROBERT COLVILE, Centre for Policy Studies

"A thoroughly-evidenced, sensitively-reported and utterly terrifying
anatomy of the collapse of our welfare state. A vital study for this
moment as the UK's safety net appears to be in maximum danger."

ANOOSH CHAKELIAN, Britain Editor, *New Statesman*

"This is a fascinating and carefully researched book, written
with Helen Barnard's trademark friendly style and warmth. She
examines the challenges of finding a new path after Covid with
the same motivation and ambition that must have powered the
original Beveridge Report. Best of all, it's a book that's full of possible
solutions, written with optimism and a real sense of hope."

FELICITY HANNAH, award-winning independent journalist

"A *tour d'horizon* of social injustice in Britain today – and a
twenty-first-century manifesto for rooting it out. At every turn, she
presses not only the question of what substantively will have to
be done to slay the giant of 'Want', but asks how can we foster the
political conversation that is a prerequisite for getting it done."

TOM CLARK, Contributing Editor, *Prospect*

FIVE GIANTS: A NEW BEVERIDGE REPORT

Consultant editor: Danny Dorling, *University of Oxford*

In November 1942, William Beveridge published *Social Insurance and Allied Services*, the result of a survey work commissioned the year before by the wartime coalition government. In what soon became known as simply "The Beveridge Report", five impediments to social progress were identified: the giants of Want, Disease, Squalor, Ignorance and Idleness. Tackling these giants was to be at the heart of postwar reconstruction. The welfare state, including national insurance, child allowances and the National Health Service, was a direct result of Beveridge's recommendations.

To mark the eightieth anniversary of the Report's publication, the authors in this series consider the progress made against Beveridge's giants, and whether they have diminished or risen up to again stalk the land. They also reflect on how the fight against poverty, unfit housing, ill-health, unemployment and poor education could be renewed as the countries of the UK emerge from a series of deeply damaging, divisive and impoverishing crises.

As an establishment figure, a Liberal and a eugenicist, Beveridge was an unlikely coordinator of the radical changes that improved so many peoples' lives. However, the banking crisis at the end of the 1920s, the mass unemployment and impoverishment of the 1930s, and the economic shock of the Second World War changed what was possible to what became essential. Old certainties were swept aside as much from within the existing order as from outside it.

The books explore the topic without constraint and the results are informative, entertaining and concerning. They aim to ignite a broader debate about the future of our society and encourage the vision and aspiration that previous generations held for us.

Want by Helen Barnard

Disease by Frances Darlington-Pollock

Squalor by Daniel Renwick and Robbie Shilliam

Ignorance by Sally Tomlinson

Idleness by Katy Jones and Ashwin Kumar

WANT

Helen Barnard

agenda
publishing

First published in 2022 by Agenda Publishing

Agenda Publishing Limited
The Core
Bath Lane
Newcastle Helix
Newcastle upon Tyne
NE4 5TF

www.agendapub.com

ISBN 978-1-78821-397-4
ISBN 978-1-78821-398-1 (ePDF)
ISBN 978-1-78821-399-8 (ePUB)

British Library Cataloguing-in-Publication Data
A catalogue record for this book is available
from the British Library

Typeset in Nocturne by Patty Rennie

Printed and bound in the UK by CPI Group (UK) Ltd,
Croydon, CR0 4YY

Contents

Preface and acknowledgements

When a nation endures a collective ordeal, it does not emerge unchanged. Trauma brings fear, loss and, if we're lucky, renewal. The Britain which emerged from the Second World War was not the nation which had entered it. Beveridge saw the war as offering the chance of real change: "the purpose of victory is to live in a better world than the old world". The war created the impetus to re-evaluate not just what was possible but what was just. Soldiers returning from the front should not be left to the poverty and powerlessness so many faced after the previous war. Women who had lost their husbands while they kept the home fires burning and the factories turning out munitions should not face penury or see their children starve.

In 2020, we entered another collective ordeal. The Covid-19 pandemic brought fear and loss in abundance. It led to restrictions to domestic life even greater, in some ways, than those during the war. The pandemic exposed the weakness of our systems, shamefully demonstrated by a coronavirus death rate twice as high in the most deprived areas as in the least deprived. But it also demonstrated our collective strength. Improvements to social security and housing security which had seemed out of reach for years were pushed through in days. Low-paid workers, dismissed as unskilled only weeks before the pandemic hit, were revealed as the backbone of Britain: supermarket staff, care assistants, delivery drivers and many others faced the risk of infection to keep the rest of us safe. As we emerge out of the Covid-19 crisis, we have the same opportunity as that grasped by Beveridge: to create a better world rather than reverting to the old one. This book is about the aspects of the pre-Covid-19 world we should leave behind and how I believe we can grow something better.

I've loved writing this book. It's been a joy and a privilege to have the chance to do so. I'm very grateful to the Joseph Rowntree Foundation for the opportunity to be part of its work to understand and find solutions to poverty, for fantastic flexibility and support when I've been unwell and for generously enabling me to take the time to write this book.

Alison Howson and the team at Agenda Publishing have been wonderful to work with and guided me through the book-writing journey with expert grace.

Thank you to Danny Dorling, Katie Schmuecker, Peter Matejic, Gavin Kelly, Mike Brewer, Charlie Pickles, Baroness Philippa Stroud, Nick Denys, Martin Koppack, Andy Harrop and Jeane Freeman for generously sharing their knowledge and ideas, putting me right and improving this book immeasurably. I'm grateful to the experts by experience, researchers, charities and policymakers whose work I have drawn on. All mistakes and inaccuracies are, of course, entirely my own fault.

I am deeply grateful to my parents, who taught me to be curious, to pursue ideas, to debate and to believe that what I thought mattered. Finally, this book is dedicated to Ben, Ash and Orla, my constant comfort and inspiration.

Helen Barnard

Introduction

The essence of what it means to be "in want" is remarkably stable across history and geography. When Beveridge named Want as one of the giants that the nation should slay, he did not mean that citizens should have everything they wanted. He meant that people should be able to meet their essential needs. He spoke ambitiously about abolishing poverty.

So, what are the essentials for a life in which we are not trapped "in want"? For most people, in most places, a decent life means: a secure home; steady work; being able to cover the bills and buy essentials; giving our children a good start in life; good mental and physical health and access to healthcare; respect and a sense of personal dignity; feeling part of society.

What these things look like and how you get them varies according to time and place. The role of the state and the responsibilities of employers, business, civil society, individuals and families are fiercely debated. Beveridge's vision was for the state to play a greater role than ever before: as an instrument by which we discharge our collective responsibilities to one another. The power of his vision was that we can take care of one another not only through family and community but also through collective institutions. When times are tough we do not need to depend on the unreliable kindness of strangers.

In 1651, Thomas Hobbes wrote in his book *Leviathan*:

Whereas many men ... become unable to maintain themselves by their labour; they ought not to be left to the
Charity of private persons, but to be provided for ... by
the Lawes of the Common-wealth. For as it is Uncharit-
ableness in any man to neglect the impotent; so it is in
the Sovereign of a Common-Wealth to expose them to the
hazard of such uncertain charity.

Hundreds of years later, the writer Caitlin Moran (2012)
echoed him:

That's why I like the welfare state, which helps everyone –
even people with terrible personalities, or who don't know
broadsheet columnists – rather than the Big Society, which
is wholly optional and ad hoc, ie, the situation we had
right up until 1948, with its paupers' graves, workhouses,
parish handouts and all ... One of the things I particularly
like about the welfare state is the lack of admin: instead
of seeking out local, winsome widows and pressing bread
into their grateful hands, I pay my tax bill, get someone else
to source needful widows, and use the time now freed up to
watch *MasterChef* or give the kids a bath.

Beveridge's vision still inspires but our society and economy have changed enormously. The old patriarchal, patronizing
structures have gradually eroded and families have diversified.
Beveridge assumed that a family contained two, heterosexual, mar-
ried parents, with a male breadwinner and female carer. Today's
families span a wide variety of forms. Women of all classes
have entered the labour market. There are many more single-
parent and blended families. Families increasingly need two
earners to achieve a reasonable standard of living.

Beveridge, like many social reformers, came from a privileged
background: public school and Oxford educated. Prime Minister

Harold Wilson knew Beveridge well having worked for him as a researcher. In 1966, he described him as "an intellectual giant" and "an intellectual snob". Like previous generations of philanthropists, Beveridge's recommendations were developed with little consultation with those intended to benefit. His policies aimed to move the nation on from the long-established and oppressive principles of the Poor Law. He intended to establish a national minimum that was not means tested but based on previous contributions and given "as of right". But power in the brave new postwar world remained firmly in the hands of rich white men. Class distinctions still ruled, firmly intertwined with morality. Those in power laid down what the lower classes should have, how they should behave and how their weaknesses should be corrected. They assumed dependence: of women on men, disabled people on others, older people on younger and workers on bosses.

Those attitudes are not yet dead, but they have been challenged more and more assertively over the years. Modern charity and policy-making have finally begun to move away from doing *to* people and towards working *with* them. We have begun to recognize that the systems we design to support people should be created with those they are intended to help. This approach is still in its infancy, but its value is already clear. The rocky path of universal credit – the biggest change to the UK welfare state in decades – is a salutary lesson in the problems created when we design a system without placing the expertise of those with direct experience of it at the centre. By contrast, the creation of new branches of the welfare state in Scotland has been smoothed by their creators' determination to listen to people who have experience of previous systems and who will be using the new one.

The welfare state created by Beveridge has been more successful and sustainable than many predicted. It has shown the capacity to evolve over time to meet new challenges, despite repeated attempts to dismantle or shrink it. However, Want is still with us. It looks very different today, but poverty still retains a firm grip on the lives of millions of our fellow citizens. The welfare state must change further and faster to meet new challenges, including our ageing population. But redesigning the welfare state must go hand in hand with redesigning our economy, moving on from structures designed for the industrial age and developing new approaches for the digital era.

What does it mean in modern Britain to slay "Want"? Poverty wears a different face depending on where you go and what period of history you examine. But underneath the differences there is a shared foundation, just as our common humanity stretches across geographical and historical borders. Chapter 1 explores the fundamentals of what we mean by poverty in the modern era.

When you imagine someone in poverty, who do you see? Up until around 20 years ago, it would probably, and correctly, have been someone out of work for a long time or an elderly person. However, the face of modern poverty has changed. Many of those in poverty today are hard-pressed working families, disabled people and carers. Meanwhile, poverty among the shrinking group of workless families has become ever deeper. Although it is far lower among pensioners today than in previous generations, poverty is on the rise again, and trends in savings and housing are storing up trouble in the decades to come. And what of young people, especially those from ethnic minority backgrounds: those hardest hit by the Great Recession in the early years of the century, who benefited least from the subsequent recovery and who are on the front line of the Covid-19 crisis?

These are the people you should picture now when you think about modern poverty in the UK. These are the people we shall meet in Chapters 2–5, which tell their stories and uncover why so many are pulled into the depths of want, despite the plenty around them.

The experience of poverty has always been intimately connected to power and powerlessness. Privilege is the ability to avoid discomfort. Resources, material and social, bring freedom from hunger, cold, fear and humiliation. When you listen to the experiences of people trapped in poverty, the themes that leap out are anxiety, stress, stigma and a lack of control or autonomy. When you work with people who have direct experience of the social security system, drawing on their expertise to improve it, the amount of support on offer is only one element of what they care about. At least as important is how they are treated when they use the system. It is no accident that the groups with the highest rates of poverty in our society are also those that have the least power and are subject to prejudice and discrimination: people from ethnic minority groups, disabled people and women. Chapter 6 investigates the role of shame and stigma in the experience of poverty while Chapter 7 dives into the role of racial injustice in trapping people in poverty, and why poverty is so often a female burden, disproportionately landing on women.

Beveridge imagined the social evils his plans were to overcome as giants, to be slain by the Jack of a newly ambitious government. But the postwar Jack is no longer able to defeat the resurgent giants. Where, then, will we find modern Jacks that are agile and crafty enough to slay modern giants? Chapters 8–12 set out five elements of the solution to modern poverty, reimagining social security, public services, the world of work, consumer markets, housing and taxation.

But before we plunge into the solutions, let's pause first at Ditchley Park, the beautiful eighteenth-century country house in Oxfordshire best known for having been Winston Churchill's secret base in the Second World War. It was here that Churchill wooed the US representative, Harry Hopkins, to win America's support in the war. Today it is home to the Ditchley Foundation, a charity dedicated to "the renewal of democratic societies, states, markets and alliances", hosting events to build networks intended to create solutions to complex problems. In July 2020, Michael Gove (then Chancellor of the Duchy of Lancaster) gave the Ditchley Annual Lecture. He started his lecture by quoting the Italian

Marxist thinker, Antonio Gramsci, who wrote in his famous *Prison Notebooks*: "The crisis consists precisely of the fact that the inherited is dying – and the new cannot be born; in this interregnum a great variety of morbid symptoms appear." Gove drew a parallel between the time that Gramsci was describing – the 1920s and 1930s – and our own. He described Gramsci's era as a point in history when the stability of the Edwardian era had gone, economic depression undermined confidence in Western democracy, ideological polarization increased, traditional political and party structures broke down and barriers to international trade went up. Technology was expanding opportunity and changing the world of work, but new structures had not yet been invented to match these changes. Gove then outlined the ways in which our own time is "an age of morbid symptoms, with fractures across the West's political systems and a deep sense of disenchantment [among] citizens with a political system that they feel has failed them".

The welfare state designed by Beveridge has been more resilient than anyone could have expected. It has evolved over the last 80 years and survived enormous economic and social upheavals. However, it is now buckling under new pressures and is out of step with the modern economy and social mores. Demand and costs are rising inexorably and the demographics and other pressures driving these rises will only become more intense in the coming decades. Our welfare state is a child of the industrial age; it is no longer fit for purpose in a digital world. But redesigning social security will not be enough; we also need to think afresh about current and coming changes in consumer markets and in the world of work, and about how we pay for the services we want to provide.

The insights of the economist and historian Carlota Perez have become highly influential among modern-day social reformers. She studies the links between technology and social change, focusing on seismic historical changes: "techno-economic paradigm shifts". She argues that major technological break-throughs drive waves of change in how people work and live. Each wave creates a period of crisis as society adjusts. Perez charts predictable stages in these adjustments (Cottam 2020). First excitement. Then recession, widening inequality, social unrest and the rise of populist leaders. Finally, the establishment of new social norms. The state has to change its systems and role to spread the benefits of the revolution across the economy and enable individuals and communities to thrive in the new world.

We are currently in the midst of one of these technological shifts: the birth of the digital, low-carbon age. We're seeing the incredibly fast emergence of new industries, with jobs and services that were barely dreamt of a decade or two ago. Patterns of work are changing, from remote working and online collaboration for previously office-based staff, to the underpinning of online retail with massive warehouses in which humans work alongside robots, managed by artificial intelligence systems. Technology is also enabling the atomization of work, with tasks broken down into small chunks and allocated to workers through a virtual platform, which is somewhat reminiscent of the preindustrial "piece work" system that began in the sixteenth century.

The industrial revolution swept away the dominance of piece work, collecting workers together in factories and cities and connecting people and markets across distances that had previously been prohibitively expensive and time-consuming to travel. It enabled new forms of organizing and exercising power and created new social problems that the old state could not handle, triggering wholesale changes to power structures, services and the regulation of markets. Now the digital age is creating platforms for communication and commerce which are both connecting and dividing people not just nationally but internationally. Advances in technology are transforming the social issues which our public services need to address and our expectations of how citizens will interact with them. Global companies are the new dominant force in the international economy – especially tech and financial services firms – while regulation is still geared to preventing traditional national monopolies. As with all waves of technological and social change, we have to lean into the adjustment and renew our systems to match it. We must change how we support each other, how we spread the benefits of innovation and protect those are most risk of being disadvantaged, how we regulate markets and how we design, deliver and pay for public services.

1

Defining decency

Poverty means not being able to heat your home, pay your
rent, or buy essentials for your children. It means waking
up every day facing insecurity, uncertainty and impossible decisions about money. The constant stress it causes
can overwhelm people, affecting them emotionally and
depriving them of the chance to play a full part in society.

Joseph Rowntree Foundation, *UK Poverty*

When I helped set up the Social Metrics Commission in 2016, my
enthusiasm was born of weariness and frustration. Too many
meetings spent debating how to measure poverty instead of how
to reduce it. Too many interviews in which arguing over what
poverty was crowded out discussion of how to free people from
it. Baroness Philippa Stroud (chair of the commission and former adviser to the secretary of state for work and pensions, Iain
Duncan Smith) started the commission after seven bruising years
in the white heat of government, having those same arguments
but with much higher stakes.

Stroud and Duncan Smith had come into government with
a grand plan: to sweep away seven old benefits and replace them
with universal credit. They worked alongside the Conservative
peer, David Freud, who had previously advised the Labour government and then joined the Conservative-led Coalition government

9

in 2010. In his book, *Clashing Agendas: Inside the Welfare Trap*, Freud tells the gory story of his years in office. He details their battles with the Treasury through the Coalition years and then under the Conservative majority government from 2015.

The original plan for universal credit had widespread support among the policy and research community. It would have increased the generosity of the benefit system at the same time as making its structure simpler and more flexible. Sadly, this approach was dead on arrival at the Treasury. Chancellor George Osborne's grand plan for the UK's social security system was to suck billions of pounds out of it. He had no interest in Duncan Smith's vision until he realized it could be a Trojan horse to slash levels of support.

A backbench rebellion among Conservative MPs prevented Osborne and Prime Minister David Cameron from enormous tax credit cuts in 2015. MPs lost their nerve at the thought of constituency surgeries full of angry people who had seen their incomes slashed by thousands of pounds overnight. The chancellor reluctantly bowed to the pressure but consoled himself by building the same cuts into the benefit that would gradually replace tax credits over the next few years. This meant that, while many people did see their support rise as they moved from tax credits and other benefits onto universal credit, enormous numbers found that their incomes plummeted as they were moved onto it after moving house or job.

Duncan Smith, Stroud, Freud and their successors spent years locked in a yearly cycle of Treasury negotiations, attempting to beat back waves of cuts. Campaigners outside government mirrored their efforts in the run-up to each annual budget but, inside or outside government, the years from 2010 to 2019 were largely ones of failure. Deep cuts to working-age social security rolled on inexorably. These arguments were made much harder to win due to the absence of an agreed concept and measure of poverty.

Before 2010 there was some consensus around a set of child poverty targets and measures that had been written into legislation with cross-party support. This swiftly broke down and the Child Poverty Act 2010 was repealed after the 2015 election. The Conservative government reiterated its intention to eliminate child poverty but conveniently dropped measures that would show that its action drove it up. For me as for many others, it was immensely frustrating to produce endless analysis demonstrating that child poverty was rising, only to get knocked back into arid debates about what measure should be used.

The Social Metrics Commission aimed to end these wars. It gathered together thinkers from left and right with policy and measurement experts and a wide network of academics and charities to advise and challenge its deliberations. Our first task was to discuss what poverty actually was. Without agreement on that, we couldn't construct an effective measure. It was tense. What if we had incompatible definitions? Would we fall at the first hurdle? We'd committed to only move forward together. We wouldn't engage in horse trading or voting; we would stay at each point of discussion until all commissioners believed we had the right solution. Would we stay stuck at the starting gate, unable to even start the race towards a new measure?

There were passionate disagreements, of course, but it turned out to be far easier to agree a central definition of poverty than we'd feared. The "word cloud" in Figure 1.1 reflected the consensus across the definitions each commissioner had proposed. We agreed that the essence of being in poverty was that your resources were insufficient to adequately meet your needs. Those needs should be defined with reference to the society you live in; what is considered necessary to life in a rural village in Uganda is not the same as what is needed by someone living a deprived part of London, Glasgow or Worthing. And we agreed that needs were not simply those of physical survival; some degree of participation in society is also necessary.

Figure 1.1   Definitions of poverty "word cloud"
Source: Social Metrics Commission (2018).

Having started with a blank sheet of paper, the commission landed squarely in the tradition of the academic Peter Townsend, as set out in his seminal 1979 book, *Poverty in the United Kingdom*, and built on by subsequent generations of researchers. As he said:

Individuals, families and groups in the population can be said to be in poverty when they lack the resources to obtain the types of diet, participate in the activities and have the living conditions and amenities which are customary, or are at least widely encouraged or approved, in the societies to which they belong. Their resources are so seriously below those commanded by the average individual or family that they are, in effect, excluded from ordinary living patterns, customs and activities. (Townsend 1979: 31)

This definition chimes with international norms. In Europe, poverty is defined as follows: "a person or a household is considered to be poor when their income and resources are worse than what is thought to be adequate or socially acceptable in the society in which they live. Poor people are often excluded from participating in economic, social and cultural activities that are considered to be the norm for other people, and their enjoyment of fundamental rights may be restricted" (Brander *et al*. 2020).

Similarly, the United Nations Committee on Social, Economic and Cultural Rights defines poverty as "a human condition characterized by sustained or chronic deprivation of the resources, capabilities, choices, security and power necessary for the enjoyment of an adequate standard of living and other civil, cultural, economic, political and social rights" (United Nations 2001).

Poverty, then, is the state of falling so far below the living standards that are normal within your society that you are shut out of ordinary ways of life. What constitutes that ordinary way of life changes over time and between places.

The vexed question of how to establish those social norms had taken a leap forward eight years previously. Donald Hirsch (now director of the Centre for Research in Social Policy at Loughborough University) launched a new programme of research called the minimum income standard. It explores what goods and services the public think a household in the UK needs to be able to afford to live a basic, decent life. It uses deliberative focus groups to enable the public to come to a consensus about what different family types require, covering everything from teaspoons to travel.

It's not a measure of poverty – the groups are not asked to agree what people need to be defined as living in or out of poverty – but it is one of the very few solid sources of insight into what the public think is required for a minimum decent standard of living. Participants in the deliberations are clear they are talking about needs, not wants. They believe that the standard must go beyond mere survival but never stray into luxury. They recognize that people need to participate in society and have some choices but do not expect those choices to be unlimited. They do not look for what people need to be comfortable but rather to meet fundamental social and material needs, to avoid shame and harm. The groups engage in detailed debates, such as which goods it is reasonable to assume people can get second-hand and which should be new for reasons of health or quality (Hirsch *et al.* 2015).

Over the decade between 2008 and 2018, the publicly agreed minimum income standard gradually evolved. In 2008, most household types were deemed to require a landline, pay-as-you-go mobile phone and no computer. By 2018, basic smartphones and laptops were counted as necessities, partly because they had become much more affordable and ubiquitous, and partly because they enabled people to buy other goods and services more cheaply and were now more cost-effective than having a landline (Hirsch 2018).

Necessities also vary geographically. Oxford University's global multidimensional poverty index measures poverty in developing countries. Its indicators include whether a household has a safe source of drinking water within a 30-minute walk from their home. In a society where a significant number of people go without such things, that's a useful measure. In a society where almost nobody does, it isn't.

In 2019, an international study covering Bangladesh, Bolivia, France, Tanzania, the United Kingdom and the United States demonstrated the common core of what poverty means (Bray *et al.* 2019). Hundreds of people experiencing poverty were involved in the study, alongside professional researchers. The study found that the experience of disempowerment, suffering and struggle was seen as central to poverty across these very different countries. The research concluded that poverty is fundamentally about a lack of control, "leading to physical, mental and emotional suffering accompanied by a sense of powerlessness to do anything about it". "Poverty feels like a tangled web that you can never escape", said one UK participant. "Poor people are powerless in society. They cannot raise their voice because they know no one listens to them", responded a Bangladeshi participant. The study sees the experience of poverty as being shaped by "relational dynamics" and "privations". Relational dynamics covers the way people are treated by institutions and by other groups in society. Privations covers the lack of material, cultural and social resources. It includes a lack of decent work, insufficient and insecure income, and material and social deprivation: "lack of access to the goods and services necessary to live a decent life, participating fully in society".

Poverty, then, is more than just low income. It is being locked into a situation where your lack of resources means you are shut out of ordinary life and experience suffering and shame. Its core concepts are shared across cultural, geographical and historical divides, but its manifestation varies over both time and place. If you want to know who is valued in a society, who has power and who is listened to, start by finding out who is most and least likely to be trapped in poverty.

2

Hard-pressed families

It is not okay that parents are skipping meals to feed their children and it is not okay people are working two jobs, working incredibly hard and still do not have enough income to pay their bills.

Sarah Chapman, worker at
Wandsworth food bank

It's like a hamster wheel. No matter how hard I work and how much I push myself, I still feel I am getting nowhere.

A single parent

Work should be a reliable route out of poverty, but the majority of people in poverty are now in working families;[1] seven in ten children growing up in poverty live in a working family; and four million workers (about one in eight) live in poverty (Innes 2020). This is in spite of the UK's employment rate hitting an all-time high in the years leading up to the Covid-19 pandemic in 2020 and the UK having one of the highest minimum hourly wages in the world. Over the last 20 years, the risk of living in working poverty

---

1 Unless otherwise stated, poverty is measured according to the measure most widely used in UK research as living more than 60 per cent below the median income for your family type, after housing costs.

has risen, particularly during two periods of time: in the five years leading up to the Great Recession in 2008 and in the recovery from that recession, from 2012 onwards. Three factors drove this sorry situation: earnings, housing costs and social security.

JOBS AND EARNINGS

During the first period of rising in-work poverty, from 2003/04 to the recession in 2008, earnings grew more slowly for those at the bottom than they did in the middle. At the same time, housing costs rose faster for those on low incomes than the better off. During the 2008 recession, earnings fell fastest for low-income families as employers cut back their hours, but they were protected by the tax and benefit system and so in-work poverty again stayed flat (falling housing costs helped both those on low and middle incomes so didn't affect the poverty levels). The recovery from 2012/13 onwards saw earnings grow at about the same rate for low-income families as they did for those in the middle, but rising housing costs hit those at the bottom hard and swingeing cuts to benefits pulled hundreds of thousands into poverty.

It might seem strange that earnings for those at the bottom weren't outstripping those in the middle, given that the rising minimum wage meant that hourly pay did go up more at the bottom than higher up. However, workers in poverty were battling not only low pay but also underemployment and insecurity at work, both of which held down their earnings. Added to this, the positive impacts of the higher minimum wage were outweighed by rising housing costs and cuts to benefits.

Debates about working hours tend to revolve around overwork and a presumed desire for more leisure time. But for those locked in poverty, getting enough work is a much more pressing concern. Around a fifth of low-paid workers are underemployed, wanting to work more hours or to move from part-time to full-time work, compared to only around one in ten workers on average pay.

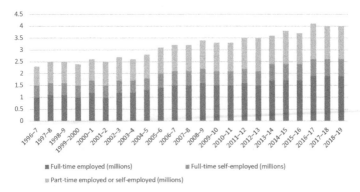

Figure 2.1 Workers in poverty by employment type

Source: Joseph Rowntree Foundation analysis of Family Resources Survey, Households Below Average Income.

For many workers in poverty, low pay and low hours are combined with insecurity. Before the Covid-19 pandemic, at least one in eight had an element of insecurity built into their work arrangements (McDonald & Sandor 2020). Their pay was insecure due to uncertain or unpredictable hours and weak employment rights: little or no sick pay, no time off in emergencies or no protection against unfair dismissal. These workers often have no idea what shifts or hours they will be working from one week to the next, leaving them unable to plan financially or organize family life. In fact, more than half of shift workers get less than a week's notice of when they're working (Richardson 2021). Some find themselves paying for transport and childcare only to arrive at work and find their shift has been cancelled. Their jobs offer little training or hope of progressing to better-paid and more secure work. They're trapped in poverty because insecure jobs tend to be paid less and because they spend more time out of work either between jobs or because they're sick or have family emergencies and have no protection. The unpredictable nature of their work makes it harder to get a second job to top up their incomes.

Sometimes it's all right, but like I've had to give my shifts away for next week because they've given me shifts that I can't do, so I've got no shifts next week and I'm only on, like, two shifts a week at the minute . . . I think if I had a job with a steadier income it would be a lot easier to save and know what I could put away each week. (Lone parent, working part time, cited in McDonald & Sandor 2020)

My contract is four hours a week but I do 30 hours a week . . . They can't offer me more than four hours even though I'm guaranteed 30 hours a week. So I don't get a pension, and when I went on maternity leave I couldn't take my full leave because of my four hour contract. (Female, retail worker, Slough, cited in McDonald & Sandor 2020)

Covid-19 exacerbated this insecurity. People on zero-hours or temporary contracts were four times more likely to lose their job compared to people on permanent contracts (Wenham & Sandor 2021). But haven't people on flexible contracts chosen them, enjoying the freedom of freelancing? Well-paid consultants might have, but many of those on low pay aren't enjoying freedom, they're teetering precariously on the edge of a cliff, trying not to be knocked off into a chasm of debt and destitution. Around half of workers on temporary agency or zero-hours contracts would prefer a permanent contract, and many would accept lower wages for increased security. Workers in the UK are willing to give up just over half their hourly earnings to get a permanent contract and over a third for a one-year contract (Datta *et al*. 2019). Holiday and sick pay are valued enough for workers to be willing to give up just over a third of their wage for them.

CHILDCARE AND TRANSPORT

For parents, the lack of suitable childcare and transport provision holds them back from better jobs. In England, only just over half of councils have enough childcare for parents working full time. Despite rising numbers of fathers taking a greater role in their children's care, this problem still overwhelmingly affects women more than men. According to the Trades Union Congress (TUC 2020), over half of mothers have changed their work for childcare reasons, compared with only just over a fifth of fathers. Three in ten mothers of young children said they'd reduced their working hours for childcare, compared with only 1 in 20 fathers. For parents working in the evenings or at weekends, the situation is even worse. Only 18 per cent of local authorities say they have enough childcare in all areas for parents working atypical hours (Coleman *et al.* 2020).

Financial support with childcare costs is more generous under universal credit compared with the previous system, covering 85 per cent of childcare costs. Three problems remain, however. That last 15 per cent can still be a considerable expense, especially for low-paid workers, reducing the gains from working and fuelling poverty. Worse, the maximum that can be claimed is capped, and the cap has been frozen since 2005 while costs have soared. And families must pay childcare up front and then claim it back. Well-off families may have the cash flow or savings to cover a deposit and fees of several hundred pounds a month. Most families on low incomes simply don't have that kind of money.

Transport also holds back parents in poverty from getting a job or a better job. Research in Manchester, Leeds and Glasgow found that transport problems shut people out of opportunities, trapping them in poor-quality jobs or making it hard to hold down a job at all (Ferrari *et al.* 2018). Many couldn't afford a car so depended on public transport. Trains were expensive and often didn't reach where the jobs were, so buses were crucial. But unreliable buses created "cut-off commuter zones" where people couldn't be confident they'd arrive for work on time when travelling more than a short distance. Many jobs were insecure and poorly paid but competitive. Being late could cost the job or lead to their hours being cut. These constraints clashed with the Jobcentre's expectations that they should look for jobs up to 90 minutes from home. Many were willing to travel for work but just didn't have affordable and reliable transport options:

> I've been offered a job and it was on the other side of Manchester and I did the bus journey to see how long it would take and it was too inadequate ... it was the opposite side of Manchester, like hour and a half, two hours on a bus, it wasn't just one bus, it was two or three. (Female aged 35, Harpurhey, Manchester)

> I was talking to my advisor, there's a place called Sherburn-in-Elmet and they have tons of work, big industrial estate but there's no bus service, it's about 13 miles away. I do not understand why they build a big estate where there's no transport, that's like tough, if you haven't got a car you can't have a job. (Male aged 49, Seacroft, Leeds)

> It could be a nightmare. If a bus doesn't turn up, you could get the sack. It affects the house and everything. I hate being late. It puts me off changing buses. Employers expect you to be there nine to five. If you're not, it's like: Right, out the door! (Female aged 48, Castlemilk, Glasgow)

SINGLE PARENTS FACING HIGH BARRIERS

Single parents face especially high barriers to finding work that offers a decent standard of living and have always had the highest poverty rate among working-age adults. At its worst, in 1997, more than six in ten lone parents were trapped in poverty. Sharp rises in employment combined with boosts to social security saw that proportion tumble to four in ten by 2010/11. Since then, it's fluctuated between 40 and 45 per cent. The fall was an impressive achievement, but it still leaves enormous numbers of lone parents and children in poverty. Just before the pandemic, nearly two in five children in single-parent families were living in poverty, compared to one in four children in couple families.

In recent years, rising poverty has accompanied rising employment for lone parents. Since 2010, the fastest rise in poverty for any group has been among working single parents. Full-time work provides the greatest protection from poverty, but since 2011/12, the child poverty rate for children in families where a lone parent works full time has risen from 17 to 27 per cent. Part-time work offers even less protection. In 1998, half of children whose lone parent worked part time lived in poverty. By 2005 that had fallen to three in ten, but in recent years it has climbed again.

Part-time work is less likely to pull people out of poverty, not only because of shorter working hours but because it restricts them to lower-paid jobs. Single parents who work part time are especially likely to be doing so because they have to, not because they want to. Six in ten single mothers would increase their hours or go full time if there were no childcare barriers, compared to only four in ten mothers in couples (Department for Education 2018). Childcare costs and availability, which are problematic for many families, pose particularly acute difficulties for single parents. The proportion of single parents who find it difficult to pay for childcare costs is three times higher than the proportion of other parents: 41 per cent compared to 14 per cent.

Having to cover childcare drop-offs, pick-ups and emergencies, plus the cost of transport, also means they tend to work closer to home, further constraining their job options. In 2017, around three in ten working lone parents lived and worked in different local authority areas, compared with half of main earners and around four in ten of second earners in couples and non-parents (Barnard 2018): "You pay the price for flexibility, you take the job you can get and fits your kid's needs, not the job you want or the career you want to reach, and most of the time, it's low pay" (single parent, Scotland, cited in Yaqoob & Shahnaz 2021).

HOUSING COSTS, HOUSING QUALITY

I'm one rent review away, one complaint away from being homeless. It's as simple as that ... it's exactly how it feels. It can't be felt any other way; that's the situation and I feel terribly, terribly vulnerable, I really do ... Absolutely, the overriding threat that hangs dark over my head; I wake up with it every day, I go to sleep with it every night. There's no getting away from it; I'm that far away from my whole world being turned upside-down. (Private rented sector tenant, London, cited in Brook 2018)

Too few low-cost social rented homes, and high rents in the private rented sector, mean high housing costs drag many families into poverty. One million low-income families pay private rents they just can't afford (Earwaker & Eliott 2021). A big part of the problem is the lack of social rented homes, crowding people into the private rented sector, especially in England. In Scotland, by contrast, lower poverty rates are in large part due to having more social rented homes than in England and Wales (McCormick & Hay 2020).

Across the UK, the leading cause of homelessness is people having to leave private rented homes. Countless policies to tackle homelessness flounder because there aren't the affordable, safe, secure homes to place people in. Many people cut back on food and other essentials to try and keep up with the rent. As well as causing poverty, people also end up trapped in homes that are poor quality, even dangerous. Because of the precariousness of their situation, tenants often can't complain or even ask a land-lord to fix things. In a research report by the charity Shelter (Gousy 2014), Mandy explained the impact her poor housing had on her son Alex's health and her own:

> Alex had so many chest infections, headaches and nausea. He had to have a month off school at one point. I have cystic fibrosis and living with damp problems meant I kept coming down with a lung infection that I'd never had before or since we moved out. Our landlord didn't seem to get that for us, the tenants, that property is our home, and a place we should be able to feel safe in, not in fear for our health.

Others found that their fear of complaining was well founded:

> I lived with bad conditions like mould and a boiler that broke all the time. There was damp in some of the rooms, so it smelled musty. I tried calling to complain about the conditions, but he just put my rent up – he said he'd done it to encourage me to leave. Finally, I wrote my landlord a letter about the conditions I was living in – and he served me with an eviction notice a few weeks later. I'm angry about my eviction and feel like I'm being punished for complaining. I'd like to fight my landlord over it, but I feel powerless to do much. (Amy, cited in Gousy 2014)

SOCIAL SECURITY: LETTING FAMILIES DOWN AND LOCKING THEM IN POVERTY

> Social security should allow people to be able to live, to be able to have enough to live on so we don't have people going to foodbanks. It makes you feel degraded when you go there sometimes. (Jon, London)

Poor-quality jobs and expensive housing were important, but rising in-work poverty in the years leading up to the Covid-19 pandemic was driven most strongly by cuts to social security. For the much smaller group of families without paid work, poverty became ever deeper and harder to escape. From 2010, two big things happened to the social security system. The first was the introduction of universal credit. The second was a series of cuts and other changes that would have driven up hardship whether they had been applied to the old system or the new. The most significant cuts were the freezes on working-age benefits (at a time of rising inflation) and limiting benefits to only the first two children in a family. These were accompanied by a range of other reductions in support for families and disabled people. The Institute for Fiscal Studies estimates that these resulted in low-income working families being on average £2,500 worse off. Families out of work were £3,000 worse off. Millions were pulled into poverty by these cuts. Others were already in poverty but were pulled further under (Hood & Waters 2017).

Some policies affected fewer people but created big losses for particular groups. Two of the most illogical and cruel were the benefit cap and the "bedroom tax", or "Removal of the Spare Room Subsidy". At the heart of these was an attempt to use financial penalties to force behaviour changes. In both cases, the majority of those affected were unable to make the changes that would be required to avoid them: poor people just got poorer.

The benefit cap was based on the simple, and spurious, justification that out-of-work families (actually those working fewer than 16 hours a week) shouldn't have a higher income than someone in paid work. The cap was set initially at £26,000 a year and then lowered to £23,000 in London and £20,000 elsewhere. The comparison with in-work families was nonsensical since a family with children and a single earner on that level of pay would get in-work benefits. Worse, the policy broke the link between assessing need and setting benefits. A family with children and high housing costs needed more money to make ends meet than a single person with a low rent. By definition, these families had been assessed as needing more benefits, but their incomes were slashed arbitrarily. The cap initially applied to around 67,000 households; by the end of 2020 it affected 180,000. The average lost income was £62 a week, or £3,224 a year. The government argued that families could escape the cap by getting work or moving to cheaper housing. However, the system already incorporated strong incentives to do both and many families were trapped in significant hardship even before their benefits were slashed.

During a 2019 Parliamentary Inquiry (Work and Pensions Committee 2019), housing providers queued up to say that they generally didn't have cheaper homes to offer families. A Plymouth social housing provider pointed out that more than half of tenants affected by the cap were now in rent arrears despite them having some of the lowest social rents in the country. Many families were already on the waiting list for social homes, but almost 65 per cent had been waiting for more than a year and over a quarter for more than five years. Shelter's analysis showed it was impossible for a lone parent with three or more children (60 per cent of those affected by the cap) to move to a cheaper area to escape it because it wouldn't cover the rent in even in the cheapest parts of England.

One of the pernicious features of the cap was that more than eight in ten of those affected were not required to look for a job. They were lone parents of young children or disabled and ill people who'd been assessed as having limited capability for work. These were groups not subject to any other form of conditionality or pressure to find work. That doesn't mean they wouldn't be looking for work of course, but it means that the government decided to jump straight to removing thousands of pounds of their incomes before trying any of the other tools at its disposal to encourage or support them into work. And they did this not only without informing them that they were expected to get a job but after explicitly telling them that they were not expected to get one. Unsurprisingly, given all the barriers to them getting a job and the fact that most weren't being given active support to do so, very few capped families got work. Evaluations found that for every 100 families affected by the cap, four moved into work because of it. The rest – almost all – were just made poorer.

The second policy was the so-called bedroom tax. Introduced in 2013, it cut the housing benefit of more than a million working-age tenants in social housing because they were classified as having an "extra" bedroom. They lost 14 per cent of their rent for one "extra" room and 25 per cent for two. Average losses were between £14 and £25 a week. Tenants had to either move to a smaller home or top up their rent from other income. As was the case with the benefit cap, the vast majority of those affected couldn't get work or find somewhere else to live, they just got poorer. In the government's own evaluation (Department for Work and Pensions 2014), most local authorities and social landlords reported that lots of people were unable to move because there was a shortage of smaller homes to move into. A detailed study by the University of Newcastle (Moffatt *et al.* 2015) found that the policy had "increased poverty and had broad-ranging adverse effects on health, wellbeing and social relationships". It affected people like George, an unemployed warehouse worker who ended up living on sausage rolls, four for £1 from Greggs, and said: "I can't sleep at night. I regularly see my doctor, I suffer from depression. If you are on a diet of sausage rolls it fills a hole but you cannot live a life like that" (Butler 2015).

And there's the woman who fled domestic violence with her young child. She was placed in a three-bed flat by her local authority, which was the only home available due to a shortage of two-bed flats. It had one more bedroom than she was deemed to need and so her benefits were slashed. Despite her trauma. Despite her child. Despite her having literally no other options. When a support worker visited the flat was freezing. The worker asked if the heating needed to be fixed, but the woman explained she had switched it off because she couldn't afford to keep it on.[2] There are disabled people living on soup because they need the extra bedroom for equipment, for their partner to sleep in or a support worker to stay in but are still subject to the benefit reduction.

These policies make no sense and achieve no purpose but cause significant hardship. They are perfect examples of the adage "good politics, lousy policy". They give politicians a good sound bite and an applause line at their party conference, but they don't stand up under the most cursory examination on policy or humanitarian grounds.

Alongside significant public support, however, their introduction was eased by the disarray over welfare policy within the Labour Party for much of this period. Labour's 2015 manifesto focused heavily on trying to create an impression of fiscal responsibility and counter accusations of profligacy with the public finances. As part of this, it promised to cap social security spending and retain the benefit cap (and even look at lowering it), although it did promise to abolish the bedroom tax. This was followed by the party abstaining on the vote passing the 2015 Welfare Act (although some Labour MPs rebelled). By the 2017 manifesto, the party had moved forward but still apparently planned to press ahead with the majority of the planned working-age benefit cuts. It pledged to reverse only £2 billion of the £9 billion cuts due to come into force, including leaving the benefit freeze intact despite rising inflation.

By 2019, the party was finally promising greater action, including scrapping the two-child limit on benefits and big improvements to support for housing costs. However, it was striking that even this big-spending manifesto committed far more additional spending to the state pension than to support for working-age families, despite pensioners having been far more protected

2   Thanks to Aileen Evans, former president of the Chartered Institute of Housing, for sharing this story with me.

from the swinging cuts of the previous decade. And there was an uncomfortable contrast between Labour's commitment to raise public sector pay, in order to claw back some of the ground lost to the Conservative's pay cap, and the absence of any plans to reverse the impacts of the four-year benefit freeze. Analysis by the Resolution Foundation showed that the manifesto left in place more than half of the benefit cuts pushed through since 2015 (Bell 2019).

Amid all these cuts, universal credit was introduced. It was designed to ensure that it always pays more for people to work than to be out of paid work. It simplified the system so that all the benefits someone gets are rolled into one and as they go into work and earn more, their social security is reduced gradually. They have a "work allowance" – an amount they can earn before losing any benefits – and after that they lose a proportion of every pound their earn (known as the "taper"). To begin with, universal credit recipients lost 65 pence in every pound, since reduced to 63 pence in 2016 and down to 55 pence in 2021. Before universal credit, there were some people facing far higher withdrawal rates, and many people faced different withdrawal rates for different benefits, making it harder to work out what you'd gain from working more hours. However, several aspects of its design and implementation caused significant problems. It is worth noting that on these issues, Labour and other parties have provided much more consistent opposition, along with sterling work carried out by numerous select committees and all-party parliamentary groups.

One of the most important design and implementation flaws is the approach to debt. If you're a bank or lender, you can't just pile debt on someone. You have to do an affordability assessment to check what they can repay without getting into more debt elsewhere or being left without enough to live on. But the government can deduct debt payments from people's benefits without such an assessment, whether for a previous tax credit overpayment, paying back an advance or for council tax or utilities. The Jobcentre work coach sets the repayments, with a strong focus on clearing the debt and no guidance or tool to ensure they leave someone with enough money for day-to-day expenses. When universal credit was introduced, the Department for Work and Pensions (DWP) could deduct up to 40 per cent of someone's money for debt repayments. After intense pressure, that was reduced to 30 per cent in 2019 and then to 25 per cent; this was better but it still removes a big chunk of money from someone already on a very low income. Two in five families on universal credit have money taken off for debt. The average amount deducted in 2020 was £70 a month, although it was much higher for some. It has baffled and infuriated me for years that the government insists on undermining the adequacy of their own system by imposing unaffordable debt payments on the poorest people in the country.

The debt problem was made worse by two factors as universal credit came in. First, the Treasury decided that as someone moved from tax credits onto universal credit, they would "realize" any debt owed from tax credits. Suddenly, people found that they owed thousands of pounds, often from overpayments years ago. This was suddenly piled onto them, despite pleas from outside and within government to write it off rather than hang it around the neck of universal credit. Second, there was a long wait for the first universal credit payment and a reliance on "advances" to paper over a fundamental design flaw. Even if everything works as intended, claimants are expected to wait at least five weeks for their first universal credit payment, but many people have had to wait far longer. The wait is because universal credit uses four-week "assessment periods" to assess your income to determine your universal credit for the next four weeks. Many expert organizations, advisers and people with experience of the system warned the government again and again this would cause hardship. The government refused to accept that the problem needed solving. Instead, they fell back on the use of "advances". Claimants can ask for an advance on their first universal credit payment, which then has to be paid back. Nearly half (45 per cent) of people on universal credit take an advance. It forces them into yet more debt, causing yet more hardship.

Poor-quality work, expensive homes and inadequate child-care and transport hem families in, making social security vital to hold back poverty, debt and hardship. But successive cuts and design flaws too often leave people "in want". Increasing numbers have found themselves relying on food banks and the kindness of strangers to survive, having been let down by a social security system that should be their lifeline at a turbulent time in their lives.

During the Covid-19 pandemic, the government recognized that the social security system had simply become too thread-bare to function, especially at a time when the number of people turning to it shot up. The hasty introduction of an additional £20 a week for everyone on universal credit was a lifeline to many during this awful period. As 2021 drew to a close, there was an intense campaign to prevent the chancellor from cutting benefit levels back again. The Labour Party and other opposition parties argued vociferously, some Conservative voices joined them (including Baroness Stroud and six former secretaries of state for work and pensions), and an incredible coalition of charities, churches and campaigners joined together to try and halt the government's intention to make the largest overnight cut to benefits since the Second World War.

The campaign achieved partial success. The chancellor agreed to a permanent injection of between £2 billion and £3 billion into universal credit; a better outcome than many had feared. But it was all targeted at people in work. Those unable to work – dis-abled people, carers, people with young babies – were abandoned and left to face the cold winds of rapidly rising prices and con-tinued uncertainty on incomes which had plummeted by £1,000 a year. Those who relied on the older-style benefits, rather than universal credit – many of them disabled people and carers – had received no additional help during the pandemic and were left out in the cold yet again by the autumn budget.

3

Disabled people and carers

I can't afford to heat my flat. I can't afford to put the hot
water on. For washing dishes, it's cheaper for me to boil
a kettle. I have a blanket and thermals on now, as I can't
afford to put the heating on.

Disabled person, cited in Young (2021)

It's strange how little we talk about the fact that half of the
14 million people in poverty in the UK are disabled or live with
someone who is. Nearly four in ten working-age disabled people
live in poverty, more than twice as high as the rate for non-disabled
adults. Comparing the UK with other European countries shows
that we are failing our disabled fellow citizens to a greater extent
than most other countries (according to official Eurostat disability statistics). We have a higher proportion of disabled people at
risk of poverty and social exclusion than all the other northern
European countries aside from Germany, which equals us. The
gap between poverty rates for disabled and non-disabled people is
also particularly high in the UK.

Disabled people tend to have lower incomes than non-disabled
people, with higher costs, pulling them into hardship. Carers are
also much more likely to be trapped in poverty than those who
aren't caring for other adults, in large part because they need to
balance paid work and unpaid caring, which restricts the hours

and jobs they can do. Young carers are also disadvantaged where their school education or chance to gain more qualifications as an adult have been constrained by their caring role. Of the nearly 4.5 million informal adult carers in the UK, almost a quarter are living in poverty. Three factors drive this: limited access to good jobs, higher costs and inadequate social security.

ACCESS TO GOOD JOBS

Work is how most people escape poverty, but disabled people are far less likely to be employed than non-disabled people and they're paid less when they are in work. Just over half of disabled people were employed in 2019, compared to 82 per cent of non-disabled people. That gap has closed slightly in recent years but incredibly slowly. Work generally needs to be full time to be a reliable route out of poverty, but disabled people are more likely than non-disabled people to work part time: 32 per cent compared to only 20 per cent.

When they get a job, disabled workers are paid 12 per cent less on average compared to non-disabled ones. Those with mental health conditions are paid nearly a fifth less than those without any disability. Part of the problem is that disabled people on average have lower levels of qualifications: they are less likely to have a degree (19 vs 35 per cent) and close to three times as likely to have no qualifications (29 vs 11 per cent). However, that doesn't explain it all: for every level of qualification, disabled people have higher unemployment and lower pay than similarly qualified non-disabled people. Even when disabled workers reach senior jobs, they're paid less for them than non-disabled senior staff (according to the Office for National Statistics 2019 statistics on disability and employment).

For Beveridge, support for people who were disabled or injured focused on physical injuries, then much more prevalent because of the nature of the era's industries (and emphasized by the postwar

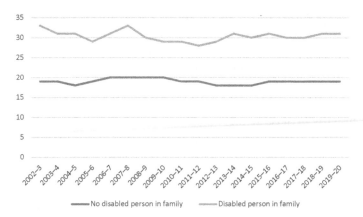

Figure 3.1   Poverty rates for all people by disability in the family,
2002–20

Source: Joseph Rowntree Foundation analysis of Family Resources Survey,
Households Below Average Income.

context). One of the problems his plan was intended to solve was
the much lower financial support received by workers who were
sick compared to those who were unemployed. But disability
benefits came with conditions attached. Receipt was "subject to
acceptance of suitable medical treatment or vocational training".
Thus, social security support had to be accompanied by "Compre-
hensive Health and Rehabilitation Services". Beveridge argued
that the logical corollary to providing high levels of disability
benefits was that the state should try to reduce the number of
people who needed it, and that the individual should "recognize
the duty to be well and co-operate" in diagnosis and treatment. At
the time, the main causes of disability were industrial accidents,
rehabilitation was a new field and many of the most common
contemporary conditions were rare or hidden. Now, the advances
of modern medicine mean that many more people now live long
and fulfilling lives with conditions that in the past would have led
to a much more limited life and likelihood of early death.

One of the reasons full employment was so vital to Beveridge was related to "injured and sick persons". Beveridge wanted all (men) to have the chance of a "happy and useful career" and also believed the income provided by social insurance was "inadequate a provision for human happiness". But mass unemployment made it less likely that disabled people would move back into work, in his view, because neither the state nor the individual would have the motivation to enable this to happen. This belief in the intrinsic value of paid work is longstanding and still widespread. A 2017 survey found nine out of ten people believed work is good for your mental health, and four-fifths that it is good for your physical health (Kelley & Wishart 2019). But the history of employment and rehabilitation support to help disabled people to stay in work or get back into it is distinctly unimpressive.

Soldiers returning injured from the Second World War were sent to work in specially designed "Remploy" factories, intended to provide "sheltered employment" for disabled people. They were created alongside other elements of the welfare state, on the assumption that disabled people would not be able to work in the mainstream labour market. By the 1980s there were over 9,000 disabled workers employed in Remploy's 94 factories. At the end of the 1980s, the focus finally moved away from segregated disabled workers and towards supporting them into "open employment" in the rest of the labour market. The factories started to close and employment service offices opened instead, although the last factory didn't close until 2013.

This change was clearly necessary. Over the last few decades we have moved from a medical to a social model of disability. Many people are disabled by the environment around them and by the attitudes and behaviour of others. Changing those attitudes and environment can free disabled people to play their rightful part in mainstream society. In the modern era, disabled people do not want special workplaces segregating them from the rest of the workforce, as was reflected in the views gathered by Liz Sayce in her review of disability employment support (Sayce 2011): "I want a proper job. I don't want to work in a special place for disabled people" (disabled person) and "I want the same choices as anyone else – to have the career I want" (young disabled person).

But the nature of the challenge has both increased and changed since those early postwar days. As the population is ageing, more people live with long-term health conditions and more have multiple conditions. Industrial accidents have fallen, so most people with health conditions are not those who had a healthy working life suddenly interrupted by a physical injury. They live with longstanding conditions such as back pain or mental health conditions like depression and anxiety. By 2020, the health think tank the Nuffield Trust found that more than 15 million people in England were living with a long-term health condition (over a quarter of the population). About 70 per cent of the money spent on health and social care is for care of people with those long-term conditions (Nuffield Trust 2020). Long-term health conditions are also closely linked to poverty: more people in deprived areas have them and they get them earlier than those living in better-off places.

By the 2010s there were four main types of government-backed employment support for disabled people: nationally contracted programmes for individuals (work choice, specialist employability support, the Work and Health Programme); Jobcentre Plus support (work coaches, some additional help for people with complex needs and some local funding for specialist support); grants like Access to Work, which people can apply to for workplace adjustments; and attempts to change employer behaviour, like the Disability Confident Scheme.

Employment support for disabled people to get and keep jobs works best when it is highly personalized and delivered by specialist advisers with low caseloads (Learning and Work Institute 2019). However, the government has moved away from specialist provision and focused on expanding support from Jobcentre Plus.

During the Work and Pensions Select Committee 2021 Inquiry into the Disability Employment Gap, the Equality and Human Rights Commission (EHRC) worried that this would mean the support would be "generic and insufficient compared to the specific and tailored advice that disabled job seekers need". The EHRC also pointed out that the Work and Health Programme set up for disabled job seekers in 2017 was supporting far fewer disabled people than had been promised, that eight out of ten disabled claimants hadn't achieved a "job outcome" and that an evaluation of the programme in London found that it offered inconsistent support and that work coaches needed more training.

The elephant in the room through all this is the role of employer attitudes. Research carried out by the Leonard Cheshire charity in 2018 found that nearly a quarter of employers (24 per cent) said they would be less likely to employ someone with a disability. Two-thirds of those employers said the costs of workplace adjustments were a barrier to employing a disabled person, an increase from 60 per cent in 2017 (Leonard Cheshire 2019). A 2018 report by the charity Scope, based on British Social Attitudes Survey data, found that one in three people saw disabled people as being less productive than non-disabled people (Dixon *et al*. 2018).

But despite clear evidence of longstanding and ingrained prejudice limiting the job opportunities open to disabled people, most efforts to increase their employment have concentrated on "supply-side" programmes – supporting disabled people – rather than on influencing employers to open up more and better opportunities. One exception to this is the Access to Work programme, which has been around since 1994. It provides grants to enable employers to make reasonable adjustments. Evaluations show that it's enormously popular among both employers and employees and has a big impact on helping people stay in work (Takala 2020). In theory it's available to the one in five people who have barriers to work because of a disability. However, it's known as the government's "best kept secret" with costs kept down by ensuring that few people hear about it.

One attempt to change attitudes is the Disability Confident Scheme, launched in 2016. It is an accreditation system aiming to help employers develop the skills and confidence to hire, retain and develop workers with disabilities and long-term health conditions. Over 20,000 employers signed up to the scheme, covering about 11 million workers. However, doubt has been cast over the scheme's effectiveness, especially given how much self-assessment it involves. The government declined to carry out much evaluation of its effectiveness. In 2018, a survey of 600 employers in the scheme found that only half had employed a disabled person since joining. The most common recruitment activities were promoting having joined the scheme and ensuring that staff involved in recruitment had "appropriate disability equality awareness" (which just under four in ten had done) (Department for Work and Pensions 2018). This hardly seems adequate to meet the challenge of changing employer attitudes and removing discrimination against disabled workers.

HIGHER COSTS AND
INADEQUATE SOCIAL SECURITY

The pressure of living on a lower income is exacerbated by the extra costs faced by many disabled people. Research by the charity Scope in 2019 found that, on average, disabled people face extra costs of £583 per month, accounting for about half of their income (John *et al.* 2019). Costs can be much higher though: one in five disabled people face extra costs of more than £1,000 a month. Lower employment rates, lower pay and extra costs mean social security is especially vital to protect disabled people and those who care for them. Unsurprisingly, the drive to cut the benefits bill from 2010 onwards affected disabled people especially harshly. At the time there was also less opposition to it than might have been expected, as has been discussed: for example, the Labour Party's abstention from the vote on the Conservative's 2015 Welfare Bill (although significant numbers rebelled against this directive from their then leader Harriet Harman). The opposition did move faster to increase their opposition to disability benefit cuts than was the case in relation to other areas, however. By 2017, the Labour Party were promising to repeal these cuts, as well as the bedroom tax (with its disproportionate impact on disabled people), and by 2019 they were promising some rises in support.

Inside government, it was cuts to disability benefits that finally drove Iain Duncan Smith to resign as work and pensions secretary, after hanging on as his universal credit brainchild was eviscerated. Over ten years, changes to social security led to disabled people losing on average £1,200 from their annual income (Disability Benefits Consortium 2019). They were hit far harder than non-disabled people (who lost on average £300 per year). Those with more disabilities lost even more: someone with six or more disabilities lost more than £2,100 per year, compared to £700 per year for someone with one disability. The very worst losses affected families with both a disabled adult and a disabled child, who lost on average £4,300 per year. When the UK's first official food insecurity statistics were published in 2021 by the DWP, they revealed, shockingly, that households with a disabled person were more than twice as likely to be unable to afford enough food as those without a disabled person.

In her book, *Crippled: Austerity and the Demonization of Disabled People*, the journalist Frances Ryan documents the appalling consequences of these policies. Ryan introduces us to Susan, a wheelchair user with a severe spinal condition. Cuts to benefits after 2013 left her having to survive by eating just cereal as she was unable to afford the food her doctor recommended, with her weight plummeting. She couldn't afford to go out, to put her heating on or use the oven. Ryan documents the deaths of people who had missed a couple of Jobcentre meetings, had their benefits "sanctioned" (cut for a fixed period of time) and were unable to buy food or keep the fridge on for insulin.

During the Covid-19 pandemic, disabled people and carers were excluded from the additional support offered to those depending on social security. At that point, most disabled people and carers still received the old-style "legacy benefits" rather than universal credit. Despite clear evidence that disabled people and carers faced much higher costs, the loss of other sources of support and even greater barriers to work than previously, the government steadfastly resisted calls to offer additional help. Their answer was always that disabled people could ask to move to universal credit if they wanted to receive the extra money. In fact, there were some hopes that the temporary boost to universal credit might persuade more people to switch, speeding up the government's goal of getting everyone onto it. These airy suggestions showed a deep ignorance of the realities of life for those disabled people and their carers.

Taken as a whole, the move to universal credit created more winners than losers (just). But there were still millions of people who would face a drop in income, sometimes of thousands of pounds. More deep-seated than the straightforward economics, though, was the fear engendered by a traumatic and unpredictable assessment regime.

A 2018 report by the Commons Work and Pensions Select Committee uncovered appalling patterns of inaccurate assessments, which sometimes seemed to deliberately ignore or misrepresent disabled people's situations. One person's report said that she could walk her dog, despite her not owning one and being hardly able to walk. Another person had been in bed during the assessment but was described as having "risen from a chair without any difficulty". One claimant was asked when they had "caught" Down's syndrome. Research by the charity Mind described both the inaccuracies and the trauma caused by these assessments (Manji 2020):

I had a face-to-face assessment and, having read through the notes made at the assessment, I can honestly say that most of them were completely inaccurate. The assessor claimed I had made statements that I definitely did not make, that I did several things during the day that I never do. They said that I leave my house every single day when it's actually fortnightly at most. They had invented an entire daily routine for me that I didn't have! It was all completely false, and I don't know where this information came from, because it wasn't from me. (Kate)

I was having an anxiety attack during the assessment. I had chest pains and was sweating profusely with pins and needles in my arm. The person didn't seem particularly bothered how I was presenting and indicated on report I was "mildly anxious". The report came back with so many inaccuracies it was ridiculous. It had no mention that I had a support worker with me, and because I drove my daughter to school, I was deemed fit. (Liz)

The treatment of some people with suicidal thoughts stands out especially:

The worst bit is being asked to tell the assessor "Why haven't you killed yourself yet? What is stopping you from trying to kill yourself now?" I get asked that question at every assessment in those exact words, even at times when I was actively suicidal. All this does is make you question why exactly. When you are trying not to think about going through with it, the last thing you need is for a stranger to ask you to go into detail about it. It has pushed me closer to the edge in the past as I couldn't actually think of a reason not to do it! (Sarah)

It is hard to imagine how anyone could ask these questions or behave with such a lack of compassion. It must be terrifying to know that your only way to have enough money to live on is to keep going through these assessments, each time wondering if this will be the one that tips you over the edge.

Enormous numbers of people go through this damaging process only to lose the support which keeps them just about afloat. Between 2013 and 2018, nearly a million people challenged the outcome. Although the majority of those who challenge decisions have them overturned either at the "mandatory reconsideration" stage or at a tribunal, they can be left for weeks or months without the basics of life. It is hard not to see a connection between the deficiencies in the assessment regime and the goal of successive governments to reduce the benefits bill.

The legacy of fear and distrust that this has created among disabled people is difficult to overestimate. It is proving to be a serious challenge in Scotland, where the introduction of a new social security system for Disability Assistance payments has the potential to help disabled people escape poverty but only if it fulfils the promise of taking a different approach. The Scottish government has a strong commitment to deliver its newly devolved social security system with the values of dignity, fairness and respect. This has been widely welcomed, but advisers and disabled people warn that changing the culture of welfare provision and rebuilding trust with claimants is a mammoth undertaking (Young 2021): "You can't overstate people's anxieties and fears about making applications ... there's years and years of negative experiences and people feeling humiliated, you know, embarrassed and challenged about applying for benefits and that now permeates the culture" (welfare rights adviser).

The idea that disabled people would volunteer to be reassessed for a new benefit, to face that trauma and risk, could only be viewed as reasonable by someone who lacked any insight into how the system is experienced by many of those who are forced into it. So how was this possible? How did we, as a society that prides itself on being compassionate and just, get here?

In some ways, disabled people in poverty or claiming social security are viewed much more sympathetically than those who aren't disabled. Even during periods when overall attitudes towards people on benefits were hostile, there was often strong support for additional spending on both pensions and benefits for disabled people. And yet, in the 2010s, when the government was determined to cut billions of pounds from social security (and to legitimize it by demonizing those who would be losing out), there were endless stories about people claiming disability benefits being unmasked as fakes when they were photographed doing something that didn't "look disabled". It succeeded because it chimed with deep-seated beliefs in much of society. Despite the surface sympathy, people often remark that, of course, disabled people should be supported, *as long as they are really disabled*.

There is a strong sense that people claiming to be disabled need to be policed to ensure that they aren't taking advantage of the (meagre) support available. I remember one partially sighted woman saying that strangers abused her in the street for using a mobile phone. Their ignorance of the ways mobile phones can be used specifically to help partially sighted people was joined to a belief that it was their moral right to check that a stranger in the street was not pretending to be disabled. Of course, many disabilities are invisible. In fact, the two most common conditions among people on health-related benefits are both generally invisible: back and other muscular-skeletal conditions and mental health conditions. Many other debilitating conditions mainly manifest through pain and fatigue. These can be overwhelming but are often dismissed by both the medical profession and wider society. The lack of understanding among employers, colleagues and friends can make daily life even more of a struggle, on top of that caused by the condition itself. Asking for reasonable adjustments at work is daunting even if they conform to a stereotype people recognize. But a discussion about installing a ramp or accessible toilets remains more familiar territory than trying to explain the more subtle changes needed by someone with fluctuating mental health or debilitating fatigue or pain.

This undercurrent of suspicion is one strand of the broader prejudice and hostility facing disabled people. The Office for National Statistics finds that disabled people are much more likely than non-disabled people to be a victim of a crime, and disabled adults are more than twice as likely to suffer domestic abuse than those who aren't disabled. In 2018 (the most recent data available) there were 52,000 disability hate crimes in England and Wales.

The last decade has been marked by highly effective action to reduce disabled people's incomes and make the process of getting help frightening and traumatic (overseen by successive secretaries of state and ministers, including Iain Duncan Smith, despite his resignation over some of the specific cuts and continuing after his departure). There have also been some attempts to help them into work and reduce employer prejudice against them, but these have been far less impactful, well evidenced and well funded. It's hardly surprising that so many are locked into poverty and out of work.

4

The pensioner poverty time bomb

Hang on, isn't this supposed to be a "golden age" for old age? Aren't the young getting a raw deal while older generations enjoy the fruits of gold-plated pensions, a house price boom and generous state support? Yes, but not all pensioners are sitting pretty and enjoying a healthier and wealthier retirement than could have been imagined by previous generations, or than is likely to be on offer for their grandchildren. There are hundreds of thousands who are suffering and see no way out.

A 2013 report for the DWP (Kotecha 2013) included descriptions of the experiences of older people living on low incomes. Despite the dispassionate language, they show the dire situations some found themselves trapped in:

> Nathan is 68 years old and has worked in various manual professions all his life – his last job was as a self-employed pallet provider for building sites. He is now divorced and finds himself living alone in social housing with an income of £120 per week. Nathan is also a diabetic, which means he has to eat regularly and to have good quality fruit and vegetables. Nathan feels his income does not allow him to do this; he can only afford to have two meals a day and cannot afford to buy the quality of meat and vegetables he needs. He knows that it is vital to manage his blood glucose

levels and does this by supplementing meals with frequent intakes of cheap, sugary tea. He feels grateful when his children come over as they sometimes help him buy groceries, but he knows they are struggling too.

Gill is in her 70s and lives alone. She has a number of health conditions that profoundly affect her ability to manage independently, including arthritis and cardiac issues. This means she often needs help bathing and dressing, as well as with her shopping. Changes in her benefits mean that she can no longer afford to have the frequency of care that she needs. She has had to cut down the number of times a carer comes in from seven days a week to three days a week.

Research by the charity Independent Age (Seaman 2020) highlights how disempowered and trapped many older people feel, especially those on low incomes. Some are physically as well as psychologically trapped, for example Omar, who lived in a council flat on the seventh floor and was unable to leave his home for 16 months because the lift was out of order.

Today's picture is still far brighter than the past. Twenty-five years ago, three in every ten pensioners lived in poverty. Getting older brought the dread of being pulled into poverty, left unable to pay the bills and shut out of society. By 2012, pensioner poverty had dropped by more than half and pensioners had the lowest poverty rate of any group: only one in eight pensioners lived in poverty, compared to nearly three in every ten children at that time. Such a dramatic fall in pensioner poverty is a testament to what can be achieved when society decides that it simply will not put up with so many of its loved and respected older members suffering under such a scourge. It was achieved by a combination of rising home ownership (reducing housing costs in later life), increasing private pensions and better support from the state. The most important bit of the more generous state support was

Pension Credit: a targeted top-up for those who didn't have sufficient private or occupational pension contributions to add to the basic state pension and create a liveable income.

The basic state pension has never been enough on its own to enable pensioners to escape poverty. Even with the increasingly generous state pension and the "triple lock" (of which more later) pensioners can only reach a decent income through topping it up with a private or contributory pension income or though other savings or resources. Before Pension Credit, this left millions of pensioners in poverty because their working lives had been marked by low pay, insecure work, unemployment or caring.

Pension Credit (initially called Minimum Income Guarantee) was introduced in 1999 with the explicit goal of slashing pensioner poverty and the government was extremely keen for as many eligible people to claim it as possible. It seems remarkable now, after so many years of governments trying to drive people off benefits, that the 2002 spending review including a Public Service Agreement between the Treasury and the DWP that set the latter a target of getting at least three million pensioner households to claim Pension Credit by 2006. The target was accompanied by £22 million spent on marketing it to claimants. I remember doing research on Pension Credit for the DWP during these years and talking to staff working in the Pension Centres. They told me, in tones of wonder, how much they were encouraged to help people to claim, how strong the drive was to get claimant numbers up and how different this was to their experience in other parts of the system.

Despite all this, around four in ten eligible pensioners (more than a million) don't take up their Pension Credit (Independent Age 2020). That means they also miss other payments that are linked to Pension Credit receipt, such as council tax reductions, the Cold Weather Payment and housing benefit. Researchers from Loughborough University, commissioned by the charity Independent Age, estimate that pensioner poverty could be reduced by five percentage points, going down to just over one in ten pensioners, if everyone who was entitled to Pension Credit claimed it. This matters immensely because, in recent years, the great achievement of slashing pensioner poverty has begun to unravel. By 2020, 2.1 million pensioners were in poverty: 500,000 more than in 2012. The rate had risen from a low in 2012 of one in eight to one in six. People often ask how this can be the case when the government has made the state pension so much more generous and introduced the "triple lock" (guaranteeing that the state pension will rise each year in line with the rise in either prices or earnings, or by 2.5 per cent, whichever is higher).

The triple lock creates a constant ratchet pushing state pensions up even if living standards across the rest of society are falling. It was introduced in 2011 after years of the basic state pension having fallen behind increases in income for the rest of the population. It then became totemic – a symbol of government commitment to supporting pensioners – even while it introduced eye-watering cuts to the incomes of other groups with much higher poverty rates. Ironically, the triple lock on the state pension does little to protect pensioners from poverty (despite enjoying very wide political support across the parties), as Baroness Ros Altman, a Conservative peer and former pensions minister, has argued (Altman 2020). It provides the most protection to younger pensioners (who are already less likely than older pensioners to live in poverty). Those under 70 have their new state pension of £175.20 protected, while the over-70s only have their Basic Pension of £134.25. Even worse, the triple lock doesn't apply at all to Pension Credit, which is the crucial bit of the system for poorer pensioners. Increasing the state pension in line with long-term trends in earnings would ensure this part of pensioners' incomes kept up with living standards across the rest of society. It would be cheaper and more logical to then provide additional boosts to Pension Credit to ensure that poorer pensioners didn't lose out to high inflation or other factors.

The debate about the state pension often obscures something equally important to current and future pensioner poverty: what kind of homes people live in. Poorer pensioners spend much more on housing costs than richer pensioners, even when you take into account the help some get from housing benefit. One reason is that richer pensioners generally own their own home, but poorer pensioners are still renting. In 2018, home owners were spending on average £18 per week on housing costs; those renting privately spent £122 per week and social renters (in council or housing association homes) spent £55 per week. Since 2012, housing costs for most pensioners have stayed pretty flat but those for the poorest quarter of pensioners have shot up (Bourquin *et al*. 2019).

Poverty rates have thus always been much lower for pensioners who own their own homes than for those who rent. In 2011, one in ten home-owning pensioners were in poverty, compared to a quarter of those in social rented homes and nearly three in ten private-renting pensioners. Poverty rates for all those groups have since risen, but by far more for renters than owners. By 2020, one in seven home-owning pensioners were in poverty, but rates for renters had risen to nearly four in ten.

This situation is set to get much worse in the decades to come. In 2022, almost three-quarters of the over-65s own their house outright. But home ownership levels peaked at the start of the 2000s and then declined until around 2016, with only a very small uptick since then. Since the early 1990s the big trend in housing has been the rise in private renting: in 1993, one in ten working-age people rented privately, in 2022 it's a quarter. Private renting is rising in every age group, but the biggest increases are among people in mid-life, between 35 and 44. This group are three times more likely to rent than was the case 20 years ago. By contrast, the proportion of people who own with a mortgage has tumbled: in 1997 more than two-thirds of people aged 35–44 had a mortgage, by 2017 it was only half. People who can't get a mortgage to buy their own home in mid-life are very unlikely to reach

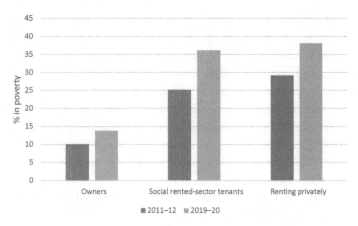

Figure 4.1   Pensioner poverty by tenure, 2011–12 and 2019–20
Source: Family Resources Survey, Households Below Average Income.

retirement having paid it off. A plethora of government schemes
to increase home ownership have done little, especially for those
facing unaffordable private rents. Most of these home ownership
schemes are unaffordable for nine out of ten low-income families
in the private rented sector (Earwaker & Baxter 2020). The only
policy that has ever successfully increased home ownership for
those on low incomes is the right to buy their council homes. But
that conveyer belt to ownership was brought to a shuddering halt
by the failure to replace the social homes that had been sold.

Rising poverty among workers and children thus creates a
ticking time bomb of pensioner poverty. Many families on low
incomes are building up debt, running out of savings and feeling
closer to homelessness than home ownership. They can't afford
to get onto the housing ladder. Successive governments have
failed to build enough social housing while continuing to sell off
existing low-cost homes without replacing them. So, more and
more are crowded into the private rented sector, coping with sky-
high rents, damp, overcrowded living conditions and constant
insecurity. That makes for a more miserable existence now and

closes down their escape route to a more comfortable later life. If you can't keep up with the bills and put food on the table, you're highly unlikely to be able to save for a deposit.

It's estimated that by 2025, more than half of people under 40 will be living in private rented homes. Over the next 20 years, the number of older people living in the private rented sector is likely to increase from just over 300,000 to around 550,000. If we want to defuse this ticking time bomb, we need to get serious about reducing working-age poverty and building social housing.

The looming explosion is given extra dynamite by uneven patterns of pension saving, despite the resounding success of auto-enrolment which was introduced in 2012, automatically enrolling most employees in a workplace pension scheme unless they opted out. By 2018, nearly nine in ten workers saved through their employer's pension, having shot up from just over half, according to the Pensions Regulator. The increase has been greatest among lower earners, but they still lag behind better-off workers. Only 79 per cent of the lowest-earning employees are saving for a pension, compared to 93 per cent of high earners. Plus, the amounts those low earners save remain pretty meagre. Even more worrying, while the number of people who are self-employed has been rising (up to five million by the end of 2019) their rates of pension saving have collapsed. It was bad enough that only 27 per cent were saving for a pension in 2008; by 2018 that had dropped to only 15 per cent.

So, we face a future in which huge numbers of people will reach retirement with no private pension or a very small one while still having to pay exorbitant rents, with no end in sight. That will pile pressure onto the state support those people will need. It will come at a time when the whole shape of our population is changing, with fewer workers and more pensioners. Extending our working lives is one inevitable consequence. Most of us know we will have to work for longer than previous generations. That's not too scary for well-off, healthy office workers. It's an entirely different matter for workers in poverty, doing physically demanding jobs, in poorer health, with a much shorter healthy life expectancy. Even with longer working lives, however, the tax base of workers is likely to shrink relative to the population of retirees and disabled people they will need to support. New ways to tax wealth and business will play an important role in cutting this Gordian knot. But we are still facing a return of the spectre of poverty stalking old age unless we turn back the tide of in-work poverty and sort out our dysfunctional housing market.

5

Young, Black and held back

A piece of advice: if you're going to live through a deep recession, do your very best not to be a young adult. If you must be young, don't be Black (or Pakistani or Bangladeshi). If you insist on being both young and Black, try your very hardest to have well-off parents.

I remember being told years ago that children and young adults are much less likely to be seriously hurt by a fall than older ones. They're more flexible and more resilient than older adults whose bones are more brittle and muscles less elastic. The younger you are the more quickly and easily you bounce back. Sadly, the opposite seems to be true of young adults and recessions.

In 2011, a young man called Marc took part in the Poverty and Social Exclusion research project in the UK (Poverty and Social Exclusion 2013). He was 19, lived in Redcar in North Yorkshire and had been looking for work for two years. He'd applied for hundreds of jobs and been on umpteen employability schemes but had no luck. In his area there were 5,490 people on jobseeker's allowance and looking for work but only 460 vacancies. He lived with his sister in charity-supported housing but only had four months left on his tenancy there. Marc talked about his hopes for the future and his struggles both materially and with his mental health:

I'll probably want in my life just to be stable enough to feed myself and my kids, cos my Mum couldn't when ... she couldn't afford to feed herself when she was feeding us ...

Some days she couldn't afford to feed us and herself so she would feed us and she would starve herself for two days. Just things like that. That would really affect someone. I wouldn't want to bring up someone like that. I would struggle. I don't know how she went through it at all ...

I've been searching for work for two and a half years, near enough three, and it's coming up clueless at the moment. Must have been hundreds, hundreds of jobs I've applied for in the past two/three years. Bar tending jobs, cleaning jobs. Everything you can probably think of, even fixing lampposts ...

Joint tenancy is really just a temporary one-year tenancy agreement house so after the year's up I'll have to find somewhere for myself. At the moment I'm comfortable how I am but it's still ticking on my mind. Because anything these days can get turned upside down and you could be out on your ... out on the streets with your black bags again. Yeah, I do kind of worry about that ...

That's all I want. Decent transport, decent house, a nice family and a decent job as well. And that's it ... Struggling means basically, to me, some days I have quite a bit of food, some days I don't, but basically that's it ...

Christmas presents – last year I couldn't even afford to get my Mum a Christmas present cos I didn't have the money to and I felt really guilty. It does take a lot out of you. I may not show it but it does. It's not physically, it's just in your head ... cos you have to constantly think about money, constantly think about it ...

Last year I had a mental breakdown in my Mum's back garden cos I couldn't hack it. I couldn't do it. I just couldn't ... I just couldn't deal with all the stress and worrying about money and everything, I just really couldn't, all the stress from worrying about money, food on the table, heating, bills, I just couldn't do it.

In 2016, three in ten young people (aged 14–24) lived in poverty, their risk of poverty had grown and they were particularly at risk of very deep poverty (Joseph Rowntree Foundation 2016). Young men under 25 were the group at highest risk of destitution.

A survey carried out by the Young Women's Trust in 2019 found almost four in ten young women faced a "real struggle" to make their money last to the end of the month, with even greater difficulties facing Black and ethnic minority young women (Young Women's Trust 2020). Young mums faced particularly stark difficulties, with half having skipped meals at least once a week to provide for their children.

The labour market and social security system drive this high poverty and also create significant gaps between the prospects of young people from different ethnic groups.

YOUNG PEOPLE AND WORK

Research carried out by the EHRC looked at how young people had done between 2008 and 2013 (Equality and Human Rights Commission 2015). Then the Social Mobility Commission examined progress between 2013 and 2020 (Social Mobility Commission 2020). Neither makes for cheering reading.

Between 2008 and 2013, more young people gained qualifications than ever before, but their employment prospects and pay had declined and more lived in poverty. Young people (aged 16–24) had seen a larger fall in employment than older age groups. Their hourly earnings had gone down from £7.40 an hour to £6.70 an hour. The percentage living in poverty had risen from 27.8 per cent to 30.5 per cent. They were more likely to live in overcrowded homes than any other age group: in England, more than one in ten

(11 per cent) were overcrowded, compared to between 0.5 per cent and 6.4 per cent for every other age group.

From 2013 on, disadvantaged young people were staying in education longer, more were going on to university and more were in work than ever before. However, this was not translating into decent living standards; young people from disadvantaged backgrounds were at greater risk of getting stuck in low-paid jobs. Unsurprisingly, the commission's 2020 social mobility barometer survey found that young people felt they were better educated than their parents but were doing worse than their parents in careers, income and housing.

Young people from some ethnic groups, particularly Black, Pakistani and Bangladeshi people, face higher unemployment and lower pay than those from other ethnic groups. This pattern is exacerbated by the impacts of successive recessions which shape the opportunities and living standards of young people, not just at the time but for years afterwards. Recessions impact especially heavily on young people. Those from Black, Pakistani and Bangladeshi backgrounds tend to see the biggest rises in unemployment and the slowest falls. The Office for National Statistics examines young people's unemployment over time by comparing the white group with "other than white" (grouping those from ethnic minority groups together because sample sizes are too small to compare each ethnic group by age over time). It shows that unemployment was already higher among the "other than white" group in 2004. It rose to over a third by 2013 before falling to a fifth in 2019, which was still nearly double the unemployment rate for white young people. More detailed analysis by individual ethnic groups shows that this primarily reflects the much higher rates among the Black, mixed, Pakistani and Bangladeshi groups.

The financial hit young people take during recessions isn't short-lived: there is "economic scarring" for years after the recovery has kicked in. Like the initial unemployment, the "scarring" impacts more heavily on those from Black, Pakistani and

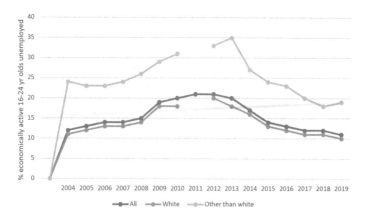

Figure 5.1 Youth unemployment by ethnicity, 2004–19
Source: Office of National Statistics analysis of Annual Population Survey.

Bangladeshi backgrounds. People from these groups are much more likely to be unemployed after the recession than white people with similar employment histories (Li & Heath 2018). Once they are back in work, the "scarring" reduces their earnings, and this impact is also greater for those from Black, Pakistani and Bangladeshi groups than for similar white workers.

The 2008 recession brought slightly lower increases in unemployment than previous recessions but a much deeper pay squeeze: the biggest since the Napoleonic Wars (Clarke 2019). Most young people who left education during this time could find jobs, but they were much more likely to go into low-paid work than those leaving university either before or after them. The impact of that funnelling into low-paid work has big implications for their chances of escaping poverty later and of their children growing up in poverty. It has become much harder for people to move up from low-paid jobs to better-paid ones. Most low-paid workers are still stuck on low pay a decade later. And they are much more exposed to the next economic shock, as we saw during the Covid-19 recession when job losses were heavily concentrated among these workers. They are also more exposed to seeing their jobs disappear as automation increases (Office for National Statistics 2019) and are less likely to have qualifications or be given training that would enable them to move into newly created or better-quality jobs.

The recession caused by Covid-19 was on a different scale to previous recessions, with a much faster and bigger contraction of the economy. Following the pattern of earlier recessions, young people were more likely than older workers to lose their jobs and to lose pay and hours and these impacts fell particularly heavily on young people who were disadvantaged before the pandemic (Henehan 2021). Before Covid-19, a quarter of Black 16–24 year olds were unemployed, compared to one in ten white young people. By the second half of 2020, more than a third of Black young people were unemployed – the rate having risen nine percentage points – whereas unemployment among white young people had only risen slightly, to 13 per cent. By the end of 2020, more than four in ten Black young people were unemployed, whereas unemployment among young white people stayed at 13 per cent. Having been concentrated in low-paid, insecure jobs, and in the sectors most exposed to the pandemic shut-downs, young Black workers bore the brunt of the economic disruption while also being less likely to be protected by measures such as the furlough scheme. By the end of 2021, the situation did look more hopeful, with young people finding new jobs faster than older workers and graduates moving into work at a normal rate (although the quality of those jobs did fall).

As well as the early economic hit, young people also suffered disproportionately from some of the wider impacts of the pandemic (Gardiner 2020). In a year in which people were legally obliged to spend much of their time at home, young people were living in homes with half as much space as those aged over 65. They were more likely to live in damp homes, without gardens, and to face mounting rent arrears and the threat of eviction. Children from Black, Asian and minority ethnic backgrounds were particularly likely live in poor-quality homes with a lack of outside space. Young people took a mental health hit along with an economic one: more than a quarter of young people out of work or on low pay said that their mental health was poor (Sehmi 2021). A third of those struggling to pay their bills – to afford food, heating and other essentials – reported poor mental health, almost double the proportion of those not facing such difficulties.

SOCIAL SECURITY SYSTEM LEAVES
YOUNG PEOPLE UNPROTECTED

The protection of the social security system is weaker for young adults than for older ones. Parts of the benefit system assume that young adults under 25 can live with their parents and so need less support, but 2.6 million live independently and 370,000 are young parents themselves. Nearly all those young parents live away from their own parents and over half are in poverty. Young parents do get more help with housing costs, but other benefits for younger people have been lower than those for older adults since the introduction of Income Support in 1988. Currently, the weekly allowance for those under 25 is less than 80 per cent of that for those aged over 25. It falls below the destitution line for single people living alone, as defined by research carried out with experts and the public by Heriot-Watt University (Fitzpatrick *et al.* 2016).

Young parents used to be exempt from the lower level of benefits for under-25s, but under universal credit support for young parents was cut. Access to housing benefit was also restricted for single young people. In 2014, the government went further and abolished housing benefit for people under 22, apparently believing that all young people were able to live with their parents. However, this was reversed in 2018 after it turned out that almost all those trying to claim were exempt from the cut because they fell into one of the groups that the government had accepted would need support with housing costs (such as being at risk of harm from their parents, having a child or having lived in care). As Seyi Obakin, chief executive of the homelessness charity Centrepoint, said: "It was obvious from the first time the policy was floated in 2013 that at best it would be unworkable and, at worst, it could actually increase homelessness and reduce the willingness of landlords to rent to all young people" (Butler 2018).

The impact of the lower level of social security support is increased by the fact that some young workers are entitled to lower minimum wages than older workers. This has had some justification in the evidence that raising minimum wages too high can lead to employers hiring fewer younger people. But overall, the most recent evidence from the Low Pay Commission (Aitken *et al.* 2018) suggests that fears of job losses due to minimum wage increases have been greatly overplayed. Minimum wages for young people have started to rise, with the age threshold for the full National Living Wage falling from 25 to 23 in 2021 and due to drop to 21 in 2024. But many young workers remain shut out of that protection.

6

Stigma and shame or dignity and respect?

Can you really die of shame? Can stigma be lethal? It is easy to think about poverty purely in relation to how much money people have and their material standard of living. But emotional suffering and shame are central to the experience of poverty. Even in the eighteenth century, Adam Smith commented that a linen shirt and leather shoes had been "rendered ... necessary" by "custom"; "the want of which would be supposed to denote [a] disgraceful degree of poverty" (Smith 1776). A 2012 study published by the charity Turn2Us divided the shame and stigma experienced by people in relation to benefits into three categories (Baumberg *et al.* 2012):

1. Personal stigma – the feeling of shame at having "failed", not being able to have and do the things that others can, being reliant on benefits or charity.

2. Social stigma – being judged by others as a failure, morally suspect, being to blame for your situation and wrongly claiming benefits or taking charity.

3. Institutional stigma – being treated badly by service

providers, feeling humiliated by the process of claiming benefits or accessing other services.

All of these come up again and again among people in poverty, especially those with experience of the social security system and people using food banks. The 2012 study found that around three in ten of those with experience of claiming benefits had experienced moderate or high personal stigma, nearly half reported feeling social stigma and a whopping 85 per cent experienced institutional stigma.

Health studies have linked these feelings of shame and stigma to increased mental and physical health problems. A review (Elliott 2016) of the links between mental health and poverty highlighted the impact on young people's mental health. It found that "chronic exposure to poverty increases adolescents' risks for developing conditions such as depression, and behavioural risks such as substance use, early sexual behaviour and criminal activity". Girls were more likely to become depressed and boys to drink too much. Tellingly, it cited the impact of "a sense of helplessness and feelings of shame and inferiority".

Many studies have documented the feelings of humiliation and distress felt by some benefit claimants, both because of media portrayals of them (social stigma) and the way they have been treated when claiming social security (institutional stigma):

Q: How are benefits claimants seen?

Alan: OK, ermm, parasites, skivers, work-shy, lazy, stupid, feckless. (JSA group) . . .

Zara: We're classed as being scroungers, work-shy, that kind of thing. All the negative stuff. (Disability benefits claimant group) (Baumberg *et al.* 2012)

As we have already seen, this can be especially acute for disabled people when they are in poverty and applying for social security support. The UK Mental Health Welfare Reform Group (which includes the main mental health organizations in England, Scotland, Wales and Northern Ireland) provided evidence in 2014 about the additional demands on their services because of the distressing and destabilizing effects of benefit assessments. Forty per cent had at least one patient who had self-harmed after their Work Capability Assessment. Thirteen per cent said a patient had tried to kill themselves and two said that a patient had taken their own life. Over a third had at least one patient who went into hospital as a consequence of their experience of the assessment.

The role of shame and stigma in physical health inequalities has also been documented in numerous studies (Inglis *et al.* 2019). Experiences of stigma have been found to predict physical ill health and factors associated with it, including a higher risk of cardiovascular disease and poor-quality sleep. The feelings of shame and embarrassment that are often experienced in situations that make someone's poverty clear to others are linked to what scientists call "identity threat", which happens when people feel at risk of being evaluated negatively by others. This causes biological responses including inflammatory and hormonal changes such as increased cortisol activation (the "stress hormone"). These are linked to a range of health problems and risks. This is of particular concern because many people in poverty do not experience this occasionally but frequently and over long periods of time.

The shame and stigma that people in poverty experience comes from a range of sources. Media portrayals of people on low incomes and people claiming benefits are often cited as vitally important by those living in these situations. Seeing and hearing themselves described in incredibly negative terms is distressing and humiliating in itself and builds the sense that those who they meet in everyday life will judge them harshly for their situation.

The portrayal of people claiming benefits as fraudsters, skivers and scroungers has a long history. A horrifying story took place in 1982 but has felt all too current for much of the last 20 years:

> In November a Yorkshire villager became the target of repeated attacks by his neighbours. Tiles were ripped from his roof, squibs were posted through his letterbox, and in the street he was subjected to constant abuse. The villager, who was crippled with rheumatoid arthritis, had made the mistake of doing some light gardening while, as his neighbours well knew, he was receiving unemployment benefit. He was just one of thousands who became victims of a mounting hysteria that in the ensuing period created a welfare backlash of cruel and massive proportions. (Baumberg *et al.* 2012)

Although longstanding, the negative portrayals and demonization seemed to take on a new intensity with the advent of reality television series focusing on them. Sometimes decried as "poverty porn", programmes like *Benefit Street*, *Benefits Britain: Life on the Dole* and *The Great British Benefits Handout* focused on extreme and deftly edited stories of people who became national heroes and villains. They dovetailed with a ramping up of political rhetoric against benefit claimants, laying the groundwork for the sweeping cuts to social security that followed the 2015 election. Stories seeded in newspapers and dramatized in our living rooms painted a picture of people who were undeserving of support, placing a burden on "hard-working taxpayers" by claiming benefits that they either were not entitled to or could easily avoid by choosing to work, be healthier or have fewer children. The image was created of people living lives of luxury, unavailable to those who worked and did not claim benefits. One of the oddest symbols of this supposed taxpayer-funded plenty was repeated references in a 2012 story to a family on benefits who had "luxury parrots" (presumably as opposed to the economy parrots, which any sensible person would confine themselves to if money was tight).

These kinds of portrayals of people on benefits, or in poverty, or in social housing do not only affect the self-esteem and emotional well-being of those being described, they also facilitate cuts to services and poor treatment by service providers. I've spoken to many people who feel that they have been treated disrespectfully or ignored by service providers, from doctors' receptionists to Jobcentre staff and housing associations because of assumptions about them. Disabled people are under suspicion for exaggerating their health problems, unemployed people are assumed to be lazy and lone parents are judged for their presumed sexual history.

The academic Tracy Shildrick examines these issues in relation to the worst fire in Britain for decades: the Grenfell Tower fire (Shildrick 2018). One of the most shocking revelations about the lead-up to that disaster was that the residents of Grenfell had warned the council about the dangerous conditions for a long time but were ignored. In November 2016, less than a year before the fire, the residents' Grenfell Action Group had said "it is a truly terrifying thought but the Grenfell Action Group firmly believe that only a catastrophic event will expose the ineptitude and incompetence of our landlord". This was an especially tragic case, but it is not an isolated one. The ease with which people in poverty are ignored when they complain or raise concerns about fundamental issues of safety or service speaks to the sense of them being seen as unimportant, powerless and not deserving of respect or consideration.

In 2021, the ITV journalist Daniel Hewitt spent months documenting the appalling living conditions endured by people in some social housing. He uncovered multiple homes with mould, leaks, no lights, rodent infestations and collapsed ceilings. Residents had complained for many months, or even years, but were ignored. These were not "rogue landlords" with a couple of properties; they included large, well-established housing associations such as Clarion Housing, which has 125,000 homes across the UK and a turnover of £943 million.

> Juliet Amedline works two jobs to pay for a Clarion flat that is falling apart. The kitchen ceiling is covered in black mould, and there are huge holes in the walls that she has been forced to cover herself with cardboard and gaffer tape to stop rodents coming in. She has even bought a bag of cement herself and filled in holes in the walls after Clarion failed to fix them. Janet says the sound of rats moving around in her walls prevents her from sleeping [at] night. Her bathroom is also rotting – the door and bath panels are broken, chunks of plaster have fallen from the walls and Janet is forced to wash with a bucket because the bath leaks into the property below. (Hewitt 2021)

The shame of being forced to endure such living conditions or the humiliating treatment of service providers is compounded by the powerlessness of knowing that you don't have any better options. Without the money to afford higher rent elsewhere, your only other option is homelessness. Stuck in a badly paid job or unable to work through illness, you have to accept the treatment you're given in order to access the social security support that will (hopefully) enable you to pay the bills.

Social stigma is felt by people living in poverty across many different times and countries. In 2014, researchers Elaine Chase and Grace Bantebya-Kyomuhendo published a book detailing experiences of poverty and shame across countries as varied as India, Uganda, Pakistan, China, Norway and South Korea, as well as the UK (Chase and Bantebya-Kyomuhendo 2014). They describe the deep shame felt by those in poverty and their attempts to cover up their poverty to avoid social humiliation and to appear "normal" within their community: parents in Uganda trying to make sure their children looked clean and tidy, parents in Oslo trying to make sure their children didn't stand out, people in Britain placing great weight on the importance of furniture polish and a haircut.

These attempts are rarely wholly successful, however, and one frequent consequence of poverty is social isolation among adults and children. Socializing often entails expense, which can be out of reach even if it is very modest, like a bus fare and the cost of a cup of tea. Children are often shut out of leisure activities where they could make and deepen friendships. Neither children nor adults want friends to see living conditions they're ashamed of. Both adults and children try to minimize their shame by avoiding occasions which might expose it, not mentioning invitations that could put a strain on the family budget and claiming not to want to join in rather than admit that they cannot afford to.

The sense of shame often leads people to avoid asking for help from both official and informal sources. Many put off or avoid claiming benefits. They go without food rather than go to a food bank. They avoid family rather than expose need that could lead to offers of help which they know could place additional strain on relatives who themselves are on low incomes:

> Do you know, once I went into town and I was kind of embarrassed to use [my free bus pass], I've actually paid ... Because that's the way they make you feel, that you would rather pay so that they don't know that you're not working, so they don't know that you're getting certain benefits.

> I didn't sign on for ages, I was just hoping I'd get a job. I was living off my savings and then next thing there was nothing left ... Mam always offers me a sandwich but I tell her I've already eaten, it's just ... I feel ashamed. I fill up on cereal or yoghurts or herbal tea, things like that. (Denise, cited in Garthwaite 2016)

Social stigma and feelings of shame are often linked by those experiencing them to how they are treated when they claim benefits or try to access services:

> I think the way the Job Centres treat people who are on benefits is absolutely shocking. I mean, these are the people that are employed to help people to get back to work, but they're the most likely to judge you – you're not looking for enough jobs, you're not applying for enough jobs, you need to be doing more. And you're not gonna motivate people by constantly putting them down. (Linda, cited in Inglis *et al.* 2019)

A constant theme in research on this topic are the feelings of poor treatment of social security claimants by Jobcentre staff and the lack of dignity within the system. However, it is important to be clear that this is by no means universal and that many Jobcentre staff do their best to provide effective and compassionate support. During the first months of the Covid-19 pandemic, unprecedented numbers of people turned to the social security system for support. One of the unsung successes of the government's response to Covid-19 was the way that the system held up under such intense pressure. This was helped, of course, by the move to digitalization in previous years, but it was also a testament to the incredibly hard work and depth of commitment among staff throughout the Jobcentre network and the DWP.

DWP satisfaction surveys with claimants typically find that around eight in ten are satisfied with the service they have received. However, this does not necessarily mean that none of these claimants have experienced a system which they find humiliating. In the 2000 British Social Attitudes Survey, more than four in ten people said that "[p]eople receiving social security are made to feel like second class citizens". In 2011, a poll of disabled people found the majority of people who had come into contact with Jobcentre or Employment Agency staff said they had experienced discrimination (Baumberg 2012). An independent survey in 2012 asked about whether people claiming benefits were treated with respect. Only 15 per cent said that they were, with 39 per cent disagreeing and 46 per cent strongly disagreeing.

Accessing help from a food bank or other charity is also associated with shame and humiliation. In this instance, very often the experience of the service and how people are treated is very positive. However, the fact of having to turn to strangers for essentials is linked to a strong sense of individual and social shame, as was described powerfully in a 2016 study of food bank users by researchers at Birmingham (Garthwaite 2016):

Tracey: I said to Glen "Get inside, don't let no one see us" cos obviously we'd never had to go anywhere like that before.

Glen: Ashamed, just felt ashamed.

Tracey: We were just so ashamed we had to go.

Researcher: And how did you find it once you got in?

Glen: It was alright cos there were other people in there like us, y'know what I mean?
I felt a bit embarrassed at first but at the end of the day if it's going to help me out, my health, if it's going to feed me instead of being starving for days until I get my money, then I'm going to use it. I thought people [at the food bank] were gonna look down their nose at me, not even have a smile for me, snatch the paper out of my hand but it was the total opposite. I felt comfortable there, the fact that I actually stayed there about an hour and a half ... [laughs] I think for me it was a nice experience, really.

The importance of living with dignity and being treated with respect extends beyond services and social security. One study, co-led by workers in poverty, developed a definition of a "good job" (Brook 2021). Strikingly, pay was only one aspect of what was important. Hours, flexibility and security were key but so were the relational aspects of work:

> Employers need to look after people. Richard Branson said it: look after your staff and they look after you. You need management that listen to you and understand what you're going through, that don't talk down at you. It's about being respected.
>
> Wherever you work, you need to be valued as a person not just an employee. When I've stayed in a job for longer it's because I've felt valued, part of the team, appreciated, that when I say things people will listen and take it on board – not necessarily always do it but at least listen and take it on board. Obviously also the pay needs to be good so you can pay the bills. If a job pays well that also shows the worth of the employee. (James, cited in Brook 2021)

The famous hierarchy of needs set out by Maslow in 1943 includes the need for social belonging and for esteem, both respect from others and self-respect. It is very clear from research with people in poverty and in the advocacy led by those with direct experience that these are as vital as material needs. The shame and stigma felt by those trapped in poverty damages their physical and mental health, creates social isolation and exposes them to the dangers and distress of poor service and humiliation.

7

Equality and discrimination

We have already seen that disabled people are much more likely to live in poverty compared to non-disabled people, that this is closely linked to the prejudice that still exists against them and that their social security support has been eroded in recent years. Two other dimensions of equality that are intimately connected to poverty are ethnicity and gender.

RACIAL INJUSTICE:
THE INVISIBLE POVERTY TRAP

In 2020, the persistence and consequences of racial injustice were put into stark relief by the combination of the shockingly un-equal impacts of the Covid-19 pandemic and increased activism and awareness sparked by the murder of George Floyd and the rise of the Black Lives Matter movement. People from Black and South Asian groups suffered disproportionately high death rates from Covid-19, as did people from deprived backgrounds. This shouldn't have been a surprise. Health inequalities are longstand-ing and stubborn: people from poorer backgrounds have higher rates of illness and shorter, less healthy lives than those who are better off. The accumulated stresses of poverty, the impacts of unhealthy housing and poor-quality work, and less access to health and other services all combine to produce this pattern. The

Covid-19 pandemic followed the same path, disproportionately hitting people who already had poor health, lived in overcrowded homes and did jobs that meant they were at higher risk. That led to disproportionately high deaths among people from some Black and minority ethnic groups because of the higher proportions living in poverty, in bad housing and in low-paid, insecure jobs which couldn't be done from home.

If you live in a Black or minority ethnic family, your chances of living in poverty are much higher than if you live in a white family. A fifth of people in white families live in poverty, compared to more than a third of those in Black and minority ethnic families. The patterns vary across different ethnic groups of course: more than half of people in the Bangladeshi group live in poverty, nearly half of Pakistani people and four in ten Black people. By contrast, a quarter of those of Indian heritage do: still higher than the fifth of white people but a much smaller gap.

The most important reason for the higher poverty rates is inequality in our labour market. Unemployment rates are much higher for some ethnic minority groups, especially Black, Pakistani and Bangladeshi groups. But even when in work, there is a substantial pay gap. Comparing two graduate men, one Black and the other white, working in the same job in the same region with the same education, the Black worker earns 17 per cent on average less than the white worker (Khan 2020). So, in-work poverty is far higher for some Black and ethnic minority groups than for the white majority (Joseph Rowntree Foundation 2021).

Lower incomes are matched by lower savings and far less wealth: Pakistani households have around 50 pence for every £1 of white British wealth, Black Caribbean households around 20 pence for every £1 of white British wealth and Black African and Bangladeshi households, 10 pence. This fuels intergenerational inequalities, with families in some ethnic minority groups much less able to pass on wealth to their children, with all the security and opportunity that brings. These patterns aren't explained

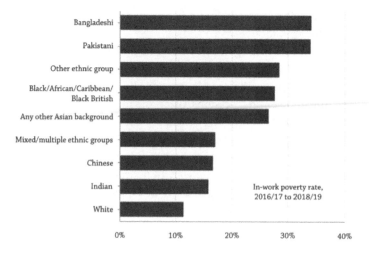

Figure 7.1 In-work poverty for Bangladeshi and Pakistani workers

Source: Joseph Rowntree Foundation analysis of Households Below Average Income statistics, based on the Family Resources Survey, 2017/18–2019/20 (three-year average used due to low sample sizes for some ethnic groups).

by education: many ethnic minority groups outperform white groups in school and higher education. Although there are still issues to be addressed in education, such as much higher exclusion rates for Black children, it is labour market inequalities that are mainly holding people back. These inequalities lead to occupational segregation, with people from some groups concentrated in sectors where low pay is common. Nearly one in three Bangladeshi men work in catering, restaurants and related businesses, compared to 1 in 100 white British men. Only 1 in 100 white British men work in taxi, chauffeuring and related businesses, compared to one in seven Pakistani men. Even within industries, people from some ethnic minority groups are more likely to be low paid and find it harder to progress up to better-paid jobs.

Greater difficulties getting a job don't only lead to higher unemployment, they also reduce the opportunities for some groups of workers to increase their pay by moving job and employer. As we have already seen, in recessions, Black and minority ethnic workers tend to be hit harder by unemployment and earnings loss, with scarring effects that can last for years. During the Covid-19 pandemic, Black, Asian and ethnic minority workers were 13 per cent less likely to be furloughed but 14 per cent more likely to be made unemployed (Dudding 2021). In 2009, the DWP published a study (Wood *et al.* 2009) testing whether employers discriminate against job applicants they perceive to be other than white British. Identical applications were sent, some with names associated with being white British and others with names associated with being from an ethnic minority group. The stark finding was that applicants perceived to be from an ethnic minority group had to send in 74 per cent more applications to get a positive response from an employer.

In 2019, a similar study was published by the Centre for Social Investigation at Nuffield College (Stasio & Heath 2019). They found staggeringly high levels of discrimination: applicants perceived as being from an ethnic minority group had to send in 60 per cent more applications to get a callback. That rose to 70 per cent for Pakistani-sounding and 80 per cent for Nigerian-sounding names. Even having a relevant degree and work experience didn't level the playing field. The researchers also compared the situation in Britain to that in a few other European countries. They found that ethnic minority applicants had to send in significantly more applications to get a callback than in other countries. The situation was most positive (among the countries included) in Spain, where there was no difference in the number of applications ethnic minority candidates had to send in. In Germany the callback ratio was 1:2: ethnic minority candidates had to send it two applications for every one a white candidate sent. In the Netherlands that rose to 1:3, in Norway to 1:5 and in Britain to 1:6.

These hard, cold statistics about racism and discrimination reflect millions of individual experiences that are part of daily life for many ethnic minority people, from childhood onwards. In March 2021, the *Guardian* published (Parveen & Thomas 2021) a round-up of accounts from children of their experiences facing racism in school. It included:

> 15-year-old boy from Bradford who says he was likened to Osama bin Laden and routinely called the P-word ...

> 14-year-old girl from Greater Manchester who spoke about being forced to move schools after her hijab was ripped off and she was pushed into a road ...

> 15-year-old boy, who described being called the N-word by his peers, before being made to give an assembly to explain why it was considered a racial slur to those same peers.

As part of Black History Month 2020, Virgin's IT operations manager, Chuks Nwaobasi, shared his story (Nwaobasi 2020) of experiencing racism through three generations in the UK. He described his father's experiences in the 1960s of seeing signs in windows saying "No Blacks, No Irish, No Dogs", of having his car vandalized and being sent to work close to a furnace without protective gear because "he should be used to the heat". He recounts his own experiences as a child in the 1970s, of fellow children being told by their parents not to play with Black kids, being chased off a basketball court and finding it covered in racist graffiti. He describes seeing women clutching their bags when they see a Black man and being followed round shops by security. He also shares his wife's experience as a nurse and the common incidents of racist abuse and threats of violence. And finally, his daughter's experience of a customer insisting on speaking to a white pharmacist and having changed her name to make job hunting easier.

Debates in the UK about race and racism have become increasingly polarized in recent years. However, as Sunder Katwala, CEO of the British Future think tank, has argued, binary questions like "is Britain racist?" obscure the nuanced reality (Katwala 2021). Explicit, overt, in-person racism is much less common than it was a few decades ago. But online racist abuse has grown and is now a pretty universal experience for any Black and minority ethnic person in the public eye. Ethnic minority people in Britain are more likely to have a degree than white British people but face substantial discrimination in the labour market. There are increasing numbers of ethnic minority MPs and business leaders, but the upper echelons of power remain achingly white. Class plays an enormous role in this: opportunities are more abundant for middle- and upper-class ethnic minority people but still far out of reach for many of those who are poorer and working class.

Labour market inequalities are compounded by inequalities in other areas of life, such as the housing market (Rogaly *et al.* 2021). All ethnic minority groups other than those from an Indian background are more likely than white British people to rent their home and to rent it privately. Only one in ten white workers spend over a third of their income on housing, compared to more than a quarter of Black and minority ethnic workers. But many Black and minority ethnic groups are still disproportionately likely to live in poor-quality and overcrowded homes. Bangladeshi, Pakistani and Black African families are all more likely to live in damp homes than white British families.

There is a long history of discrimination in housing. In the 1960s and 1970s, when Black people tried to get access to social housing, local authority housing officers judged tenants on their "housekeeping standards" and allocated Black people lower-quality homes. In 1969, the Birmingham housing department introduced a dispersal policy stating that no estate could have more than one in six properties occupied by a Black tenant. That policy was abandoned in 1975, and in 1976 Race Relations legislation was extended to housing, but discrimination continued. In the 1980s, Birmingham local authorities excluded Black and South Asian residents from social housing and from better-quality and newer homes. In 1988, Camden and Hammersmith councils refused to offer housing to homeless migrant families. When a new Choice Based Lettings system was introduced from 2001, it was intended to give more power to tenants but resulted in ethnic minority tenants being further concentrated in deprived areas and lower-quality homes (van Ham & David 2012).

Discrimination is rife in the private rented sector, where Black and minority ethnic people tend to end up. A 2013 survey (Runnymede Trust 2013) found that nearly a third of Black and Pakistani households had been discriminated against. A BBC investigation (Lynn & Davey 2013) found ten property agencies that were prepared to refuse to show a flat to Black tenants if the landlord "doesn't like the client's ethnicity".

The inequalities in our labour and housing markets combine to increase the importance of social security support for some ethnic minority groups, so cuts hit them hard, especially ethnic minority women. For instance, 8 in every 20 families affected by the benefit cap in England are from Black and minority ethnic groups, even though they make up only 3 in 20 of the population.

These policy impacts are exacerbated by some elements of migration policy. The policy of "No Recourse to Public Funds" (NRPF), preventing some migrants from accessing state support, mainly affects people from Black and minority ethnic groups. It was introduced in 1971 and designed specifically to exclude Black and minority ethnic Commonwealth migrants and former colonial subjects from welfare support in the UK. It was expanded in 2012 to a wider group of people seeking leave to remain with close family in the UK. Many of those subject to NRPF do eventually gain residency or settled status or prove their right to support, but it often takes years, during which time they are at high risk of destitution. NRPF currently affects around 1.4 million people, including 175,000 children.

The other policy that increases the difficulties facing many Black and minority ethnic people is the "hostile environment" or "compliant environment" policy. This was formally brought in as a strategy in 2012 by then home secretary, Theresa May, but had been introduced conceptually years earlier by the New Labour immigration minister, Liam Bryne, in 2007. The Home Affairs Select Committee describes it as measures "designed to make life difficult for individuals without permission to remain in the UK...The aim of the policy is to deter people without permission from entering the UK and to encourage those already here to leave voluntarily. It includes measures to limit access to work, housing, healthcare, and bank accounts, revoke driving licenses and to reduce and restrict rights of appeal against Home Office decisions" (Home Affairs Committee 2018).

The hostile environment strategy has affected not only those groups it is intended to target but Black and minority ethnic people much more broadly. For example, the requirement to check immigration status led to employers and landlords discriminating against people they think might be migrants, which in practice is often anyone who is not white or has a "foreign sounding" name. This can be seen most clearly in the impacts of the Right to Rent policy.

The Right to Rent policy was introduced in 2016 and made it a criminal offence for landlords to let to tenants without leave to remain in the UK. Given the discrimination that already existed, it's not surprising that it led to landlords discriminating against Black and minority ethnic people who they think might be "foreign". This was clear even during the pilot, when more than a quarter of landlords said that they "would no longer engage with those with foreign accents or names" (Joint Council for the Welfare of Immigrants 2016). In 2018, the Independent Chief Inspector of Borders and Immigration found that the policy did not meet its aims and led to a lot of wrong decisions. It narrowed the housing options available to many and resulted in homelessness and exploitation for some of those discriminated against (Independent Chief Inspector of Borders and Immigration 2007).

POVERTY: A FEMALE BURDEN

More women than men live in poverty, and women with children are much more likely to be in poverty than women without children. The roots of this lie in the way that domestic and paid labour are divided along gender lines.

Even in couples, despite women's rocketing employment rates, they still spend significantly more time on unpaid work – caring, household chores, life admin – than men. On average women do 60 per cent more unpaid work than men (Office of National Statistics 2016). That inequality in unpaid work helps restrict women to working part time. More than four in ten women work part time (6.3 million) compared to only around one in eight men (2.3 million). This restricts them to a smaller pool of jobs and to lower-paid roles. That need for mothers to work part time to allow time for caring is the biggest driver of the gender pay gap (Costa Dias *et al.* 2018). Before having children, the hourly wage gap between men and women is about 10 per cent. After they have children, the gap gradually increases: women take a pay hit when they become parents but men don't. By the time their first child is 20, women's hourly wages are about a third lower than men's.

The women most at risk of poverty are lone parents, nine in ten of whom are women. More than four in ten (45 per cent) of female lone parents live in poverty, compared with nearly a quarter

(23 per cent) of working-age single women without children and just over a fifth (22 per cent) of working-age women who have children with a partner. Lone parents are also much more likely to be stuck in persistent poverty.

Women overall, and single parents especially, disproportionately work in sectors with high levels of low pay – for example retail and hospitality – and those same sectors were hardest hit by the Covid-19 pandemic. Nearly half of lone parents were working in places like hotels, shops and restaurants, which saw the greatest pandemic impact, compared to only a quarter of couples with children (Gingerbread 2020). Drops in hours and job losses were much more common among single parents than among couples during the pandemic, driven by a combination of having to cover childcare and homeschooling and the nature of their jobs.

All the constraints on the jobs that single parents can take because of their childcare obligations translate into a pay penalty compared to both mothers and fathers in couples. Just before the pandemic, a third of single parents were stuck on low pay, compared to just under a fifth of mothers in couples and less than one in ten fathers in couples (Dromey *et al.* 2020). And the pay gap between single parents and parents in couples has grown over time (Barnard 2018): since 2001–2, the pay gap between lone parents and the second earner in couples increased from just 31 pence to £2.14 an hour. The pay gap between lone parents and the main earner in couples increased from £3.59 to £5.86 an hour.

A lifetime of interrupted work and lower earnings translates into lower pensions. This, plus women's longer lives, mean that single female pensioners are more likely to face poverty in their retirement than male pensioners.

The ways in which families manage their resources within the home also impact more heavily on women. In low-income families especially, women tend to be responsible for managing a very low budget and finding ways to try and meet everyone's needs without enough money to cover essentials (Women's Budget Group 2018). Fathers and mothers often sacrifice to protect their children, but it is particularly mothers in poorer families who act as "poverty shock absorbers", doing without food, clothes and other essentials to try and protect their children and other adults in the family.

The darker side of family life is also intimately intertwined with poverty and disproportionately affects women. In 2019, the Office for National Statistics estimates that 1.6 million women (7.3 per cent) and 757,000 men (3.6 per cent) experienced domestic abuse (Office for National Statistics 2020). The risk of abuse is higher if you're in poverty: a Home Office study found that women in low-income families were 3.5 times more likely to experience domestic violence than women in slightly better-off families (Walby & Allen 2004). For most women, economic abuse happens alongside other kinds of abuse (Howard 2018). Nearly all victims experience coercive control of their finances, and about nine in ten find their abuser sabotaging their work by making them late or turning up at their workplace. Economic control makes it harder for women to leave and means that, if they do leave, they're likely to face even greater financial hardship, as well as the risk of escalating violence from the abusive partner.

Shirley works with both the Joseph Rowntree Foundation and Gingerbread as an expert by experience. She was a nurse, working full time, on a decent income, with a mortgage. She escaped her abusive partner, with her children, and ended up homeless and living in a hostel. Her situation was compounded by developing a disability (cervical spondylotic myelopathy) and having to fight for the disability benefits she was entitled to. She went to a tribunal three times and won each time but was pulled into debt by the time it took to win the income she should have received much earlier. She has a water meter and costs keep going up, creating constant worry and forcing her to cut back on water usage as well as other essentials. She has to ration water, reducing the frequency of washing and even of flushing the toilet. As Shirley says: "This is my everyday life. In a decent society, you should be able to wash when you want ... Access to clean water should be a basic human right ... Any increase [in the bill] means having to cut back on other things – food or clothing."

8

What is social security for?

The Beveridge report was famously popular, with people queuing up to buy it. Beveridge was certainly concerned to reflect in his proposals his views about what the British public believed was fair and would put up with. But his blueprint and the prior reports it built on were developed in a period still dominated by hierarchy and patronage. The leading thinkers behind them were from privileged backgrounds with a strong flavour of what we now call the "white saviour complex" in relation to international development: solutions developed and delivered by well-intentioned outsiders with little or no input from those they intend to help and certainly no ceding of power to people with direct experience of the issues under consideration. Since the initial setting up of the welfare state, it has been built on and adapted over time to meet changing political imperatives but rarely with much involvement of those with direct experience of the system or other parts of the public. Even very big changes – such as the introduction of universal credit – have been pursued with extraordinarily little involvement from either the wider public or those with direct experience of the system.

This lack of public engagement has become more problematic as the cost of the system has increased and the problems it needs to address have evolved. There has been a constant pressure to reduce the cost of many parts of the system, with little or no substantive discussion of what we, as a society, really value and want to maintain, let alone how we collectively want the system to evolve to meet modern challenges. Attacking and defending specific benefit levels or conditions have consumed the debate, leading to constant changes back and forth as political pressures shift.

If we want to create a better social security system, it has to be based on sustainable public consent. That doesn't mean taking the latest poll and enacting it on the backs of people who are already facing hardship. But it does mean engaging the public in thoughtful deliberation and focusing on the underlying commitments that we want to make to each other. We should appeal to our best sides in this: to our empathetic, hopeful, compassionate selves. We should not allow prejudice and stereotypes to dictate policy. But the proponents of new ideas and radical solutions can't simply ignore the public's views.

Although the current system is not built on the kind of public engagement that I think is now required, it contains some expression of our collective values. Through social security, society underwrites a specific set of choices and life events. Through it we define what range of choices we consider acceptable enough to be supported through our taxes (including the taxes of those claiming the benefits of course). That is expressed not only in the benefits that exist but also the conditions attached to them. Social norms only exist because enough people believe in them. Laws only stick if most people think they're reasonable. And spending large amounts of money on behalf of taxpayers is only sustainable if there is enough public consent for the purpose. So, what does our current social security system suggest we believe?

BELIEFS BENEATH THE SURFACE
OF SOCIAL SECURITY

The structure of our social security system expresses two fundamental beliefs about how we wish to live: markets alone will not
provide all the necessities of life and we have an obligation to support one another and protect each other from harm.

Our social security system is designed to compensate for three
things that even well-functioning markets cannot fully deliver.
Much of its ballooning expense is due to additional market failures
on top of these. First, some people aren't able to work, for a short
time or permanently, very much or at all, due to disability or caring
responsibilities or through more extreme problems like addiction.
Some people who can work don't have jobs all the time. Unex-
pected life events create shocks to people's incomes which they
can't immediately make up for through earnings: divorce, fleeing
domestic violence, illness, accident, homelessness. The answer
is income replacement benefits. Benefits which make up for the
income someone doesn't have through work, savings or insurance. Second, markets don't create affordable costs for everyone.
It would be uneconomic and unfair for employers to pay different
wages for the same job depending on how many people a worker
is supporting or how their living costs vary. Being disabled brings
additional costs without delivering extra income to cover them.
The solution to these issues? Additional cost benefits, mainly
for children and disabled people. And third, markets don't enable enough of us to plan and save for the future. Planning for the
future, even for expected events, is hard and we're bad at it. Private
insurance can be prohibitively expensive, especially for those who
need it the most. And for some life events, it just wouldn't be feasible for a government to abandon large groups of people to the
consequences of not having insurance or saved enough. We expect
individuals and markets to meet most future expenses, through
savings or insurance. But for some major events – having a child,

getting a serious illness, growing too old to work – we accept that solely private solutions won't cut it and have a whip round. So, the last type of benefits are life course benefits such as maternity benefits and pensions.

We have an obligation to support one another and protect each other from harm. It is good for our whole society that children are able to develop and thrive, and that old age does not entail penury. Both morality and collective interest underpin a social security system that provides a bulwark against turbulence and market failures. For the most part, the perennial battles over social security aren't about the basic structure: the things that we choose to leave to individuals and markets versus the things we think need a collective answer. They are about the circumstances in which it is reasonable for individuals to call on the collective answer, what level of support it should offer and what conditions should be met by those calling on it.

CHOICES AND CONDITIONS

There are tacit answers to some of these questions encoded in the current system. For example:

- *People can end up unemployed and need some help to stay afloat until they get a new job, but they need to try really hard to get one and take it if offered.* The level of benefits and the conditions around them also reflect a belief, weaponized in recent years to drive through cuts, that people who are out of work should have a very low living standard to ensure they try hard enough.

- *Children need one parent at home with them for the first few months of their life.* Maternity leave, maternity pay and benefits for the parents of young children demonstrate our collective belief that this is important and that we're willing to dip into our collective kitty to support it. Of course, with more than three in ten babies starting their lives in poverty, it's clear we don't value it highly enough to ensure that families have enough to live on, but it does exist.

• *Mothers or the main carers of younger children should be able to work part time, but those of older children should work full time.* This can be seen in the evolving conditions set on when lone parents and main carers in couples are expected to start preparing for work and to take a job.

• *Work does not always pay enough for people to afford the essentials.* The growth of in-work benefits (on top of those included at the start for large families and housing costs) was perhaps the most significant change to our social security system since its inception. It reflected the recognition that many workers couldn't earn enough to afford the necessities of life. It also reflected a change in norms of activity and dependence. Women, disabled people and carers had entered the labour market in great numbers, but many couldn't earn enough to support themselves and their families. Earlier assumptions that women would be dependent on a male breadwinner and disabled people on family members were now outdated.

WHAT'S DRIVING UP
THE COST OF SOCIAL SECURITY?

If you were guided by public and political debate about social security and by the cuts imposed over the last decade or so, you'd assume that the rising cost of the system was driven by benefits for working-age people, especially those out of work. You'd also think that Britain had a rising number of larger families with three or more children. None of that is true.

It is certainly true that the cost has increased. The Resolution Foundation's examination of how social security spending has changed over the last few decades sets out both the rising cost and how the focus of this spending has changed (Gardiner 2019). Pre-Covid-19, benefits and tax credits cost around £225 billion each year, about 10 per cent of gross domestic product (GDP). Just after the Second World War that cost was equivalent to about 4 per cent of GDP. By the late 2060s it is expected to have grown to about 12 per cent of GDP. What that money is spent on has changed significantly. The main out-of-work benefits accounted for about a quarter of spending in 1987 but under a tenth by 2017. In-work benefits and those focused on the cost of housing and disability have grown. But the main driver of the rising cost of the system has been increased spending on pensioners, both in terms of per-pensioner spending and the number of people in that category.

Overwhelmingly, the largest area of welfare spending is the state pension. Since 2008 it has cost more than 4 per cent of GDP on its own; by 2018 it accounted for nearly half of total welfare spending. Average per-person spending on pensioners is around seven times that for working-age adults, with the gap the largest it has been since the late 1970s. The Office of Budget Responsibility (2015) expects the overall cost of social security to continue to grow over the coming decades, driven primarily by the impact of an aging population and an ever-increasing share of spending being devoted to the state pension.

One public conversation we therefore need to have is about the length of retirement we expect and how to pay for the ever-increasing cost of pensions. As healthy life expectancy has risen, our working lives have begun to gradually lengthen, for example through the equalization of male and female pension ages and gradual rises in pension age. However, life expectancy (for many but not all groups) has risen much faster, leading to a growing imbalance between the workforce and the number of older people drawing a pension, as well as the length of time they are able to do so. Some, especially on the left, argue that longer working lives will be unnecessary in a future economy that is less consumerist and more productive. But others point to past predictions of new ages of leisure which have been wide of the mark. They hold out little hope that such seismic economic changes will take place as to make it unnecessary to grasp the nettle of lengthening our working lives.

This debate rages among policy elites and political enthusiasts. But wider public engagement in the conversation has been woeful. The plan to equalize pension ages was announced in 1993, and the timetable was then sped up in 2011, meaning that the female pension age rose to 65 in 2018 and 66 by 2020. However, bungled communication meant that many women felt blindsided by the change and argued that they were left with too little time to prepare and inadequate support for those plunged into hardship by the change. The impact on the women and their families was made much heavier by the radical cuts to working-age benefits implemented at the same time. There was understandable anger among the group affected, and high-profile, if ultimately unsuccessful, campaigning by the "WASPI women". Ultimately, the decision was probably the right one, but its timing and implementation were a case study in how to create maximum pain for both individuals and politicians.

One of the challenges of raising the retirement age is that increases in healthy life expectancy are highly uneven. People who are better off can expect many more years of healthy life than those living in deprivation. They are more likely to have jobs which they can feasibly do in their later years and to have the skills and resources to update their skills and move into newly created jobs as older ones disappear. A rising retirement age is only morally and politically feasible if we also create more equality in people's working lives and health. This is linked to one of the other drivers of recent and future rises in the cost of social security: increasing numbers of people living with health conditions and disabilities, especially mental health conditions. The current system of support for disabled people is failing on almost every criterion and there has been disturbingly little progress in adapting the labour market to enable more disabled people to work and earn a decent living. Changes to the design of support and to the world of work will be vital both for individuals to thrive and for our welfare state to be sustainable. Similarly, fixing our housing market and increasing the supply of truly low-cost rented homes are crucial if we are to hold down the cost of housing-related benefits.

UNIVERSALISM, CONTRIBUTION OR MEANS TESTING?

There are three approaches which social security systems can employ: (1) universal benefits, provided to everyone in a particular group regardless of their other income or their history of paying into the system; (2) contributory or social insurance, a qualification based on a history of paying into the system; and (3) means testing, a provision based on need, usually relating to how much income someone has alongside other criteria and not dependent on having paid into the system.

The UK's system has always blended elements of each of these principles. Over time, contribution-based elements have withered and means testing has become more dominant, especially for working-age benefits (Mackey & MacInnes 2020). For those of pension age, there has long been an insurance-based approach but with a big dollop of universalism. The state pension is currently topped up with private pensions or means-tested benefits but reforms in recent years will increase the universalism of the state pension system even further over time (while still notionally calling it a benefit based on contribution).

The question of the right balance between universal, means-tested and contributory benefits is one of the hardest. For a given level of spending, means-tested benefits work out as the most cost-effective way to raise living standards. However, they also give rise to a thicket of conditions and assessments and can undermine the perceived fairness of the system and therefore its sustainability. Contributory benefits tend to garner strong public support, can be more affordable and can enable closer links between individual actions and earnings and the support on offer when someone falls out of work. However, they inherently penalize people who aren't able to build up a consistent work history, whether because of caring, illness or the insecurity of the labour market, and risk consigning those in most need to severe hardship. Universal benefits provide reliable and dignified support without a byzantine system of hoops to jump through. They don't deter people from saving for themselves or improving their own living standards. But, by their nature, they direct significant resources to people who are already on higher incomes and so are either more expensive than means-tested approaches or spread the money too thinly to offer the same level of support for those on the lowest incomes.

This set of conundrums is known as the "iron triangle" of welfare. No system can deliver on all three of the goals: to raise living standards among those on low incomes; to encourage saving, work and other forms of self or mutual support; and to keep costs to the state low. Trying to achieve these different goals is especially difficult in countries which have very high levels of inequality before any redistribution takes place. Less unequal countries still face challenges and trade-offs, but they are especially stark in the UK because of our high pre-tax and spending inequality.

So, how do we balance the role of different types of benefits and the demands of these different goals?

First, I don't think we should move to a system that is primarily contribution based. I think the risk is too high of plunging significant numbers of people into serious hardship and of that impact being concentrated on groups who are already disadvantaged, in the labour market and more broadly. I also think that a system in which support relies primarily on a consistent history of decently paid work is out of step with a labour market with lots of insecure, badly paid work and a workforce with ever-increasing numbers of people managing fluctuating health conditions and balancing work and caring. So, I believe that most working-age benefits should continue to be means tested and based on need rather than contribution.

However, there is a good case for reintroducing a significant contribution-based dimension to unemployment benefits, as was argued in a report by the Institute for Government and Social Security Advisory Committee, reflecting on the experience of the Covid-19 pandemic (Social Security Advisory Committee 2021).

One characteristic of the UK system which took many by surprise during the pandemic was the very low level of benefits on offer for people who lost their jobs. Prior to the pandemic, the level of out-of-work benefits had reached its lowest level since 1990 and was much lower relative to earnings than many other similar countries. Most other Organisation for Economic Co-operation and Development (OECD) countries offered benefits that replaced a higher proportion of earnings even for people without a history of contributions and that were significantly higher for those with a history of contributions. There is a strong economic argument for increasing the "replacement rates" in the UK (i.e. the proportion of previous earnings that are covered by benefits when someone loses their job), in addition to broader social and political reasons.

The UK's lower replacement levels mean the UK's economy is more deeply "scarred" by recessions: the hit to our economy is worse and we take longer to recover. The combination of low levels of benefit and a "work first" approach leads to people taking any job they can rather than finding one that is a good match for their skills and experience (Lindsay 2014). That leads to more people ending up in poorer-quality work and can particularly result in higher-skilled people ending up in lower-paid jobs with few prospects for promotion, affecting productivity and wages over a longer period than a spell of unemployment alone would create. The very big drop in income for people previously in decently paid jobs leads them to cut spending drastically, taking demand out of the economy and fuelling the recession. The OECD suggests that one long-term factor driving the UK's high income inequality is the impact of low levels of support during recessions (OECD 2014).

In many countries, people losing their job can access a higher level of support, often based on contributions, for a set period of time. This reduces the immediate impact of losing a job, keeps spending in the economy during recessions and enables people who are likely to be able to find a similarly paid job to maintain their home, car and so on until they find a job that is a good match. Currently, the UK's system does still include a contributory version of unemployment benefit, but it is set at the same low level as non-contributory benefits (and actually ended up being lower than those other benefits during the pandemic) and it only lasts for six months. We should reinvigorate a contribution-based benefit offering higher earnings replacement, regardless of savings or a partner's income. In a normal economy, most people with a strong work history and skills find new jobs fairly quickly, holding down the cost of such a system. Ensuring they can take the time to get a comparable job and aren't pressured to move to a cheaper area or get rid of a car would provide more protection to individuals and enable the UK to recover from recessions more quickly and effectively.

Finally, what should the role of universal benefits be? Our pension system is already moving strongly in that direction, with high public and political support for a decent level of pension and one which does not disincentivize people saving for themselves (as highly means-tested systems can do). A collective commitment to ensuring that older age does not plunge people into hardship is both moral and popular. As is the case with most working-age benefits, moving back to a contribution-led system would penalize people who have faced a lifetime of hardship and disadvantage. But we need to match this with a serious commitment to lengthening our working lives. It isn't reasonable to expect 20 years of leisure funded by a universal and generous benefit. With an ageing population, it isn't economically sustainable. To make this possible, we also need to rethink how we raise money for the system, particularly tapping into unearned income and accumulated wealth (of which more later).

What about more universalism in working-age benefits? Is universal basic income (UBI) the future of social security? I don't think so. I've written at more length about why this is not the solution in an essay for the Joseph Rowntree Foundation (Joseph Rowntree Foundation 2021). But here's the short version.

Many of the problems that UBI is intended to solve are real and need action. In particular, people who miss out on support that they desperately need and the complexity, uncertainty and lack of dignity imposed by much of the means-testing system. However, there is a long list of improvements to the current system which would deliver gains similar to those expected from a universal income. Some of the barriers to enacting them relate to cost and public support. Those battles will need to be won whether it is for incremental improvements to the existing system or to something more fundamental badged as a version of UBI. Choosing to go with a version of UBI would be more expensive than similar fixes to existing systems (even assuming various tax changes to offset some of the cost). I'm not convinced that the gains would be worth the additional cost or that it would help with the battles for funding and dignity that we need to win anyway.

The broader goals of some UBI advocates also sound good, such as allowing people real choice between paid work, training, leisure and caring. To really deliver such choices, a UBI would need to be set at a much higher level than any current benefits.

That would require such eye-watering levels of funding that I find it hard to imagine it being feasible or having much public support. There are other ways to make gains in such areas, such as much more and better funding for further education, including grants for living costs, and vastly strengthened support for carers. I also think there would be merit in a "minimum income guarantee" as is being considered in Scotland. This would guarantee that support would not fall below a certain level. The system could still include conditions and financial sanctions, but these would be set so as to maintain the minimum level of income agreed on to be necessary for the basics of life.

I do think there is an argument for trialling or reintroducing universality into some parts of the benefit system. Keeping some support for children outside the means-tested system makes sense from the point of view of women's economic autonomy and as a protection against their whole income being derailed by mistakes or failures in the means-tested system. Similarly, there is a good case for at least some support for disabled people sitting outside the rest of the working-age benefit system, supporting independence and dignity and protecting people from catastrophic failures in the system.

A NEW PUBLIC CONVERSATION

That's what I think. However, if we are to move to a truly sustainable system that commands public support, it isn't good enough for a handful of experts or policy-makers to take these decisions. We need to embark on a substantive public conversation about what we believe our social security system should achieve, where the principles of universality, contribution and means testing should apply, what level of support different groups should be able to call on and what range of choices we are willing to support.

It used to be thought that research with the public could only produce a snapshot of views, with polls and focus groups often struggling to explore complex issues for which at least some specialized knowledge was necessary in order to make decisions. However, the growing field of deliberative research techniques has shown that the public can be genuinely engaged in highly complex decisions through citizens' juries and assemblies. These complement the underpinning bedrock of our political processes. They enable much more detailed discussion and collaborative decision-making than is possible through elections and political parties, which naturally involve a complex mix of debates about different issues and about the character and track record of candidates and parties.

One of the most impressive recent examples was the use of a citizens' assembly in preparation for the Irish referendum on abortion (McKee 2018). There are few topics that are more highly charged or divisive, or more likely to inflame tensions between generations or deepen cultural divisions. The Irish Parliament commissioned the assembly in which 99 Irish citizens deliberated over five months, hearing from expert witness and personal testimonies representing all sides of the debate. They had space and time to listen to each other, reflect and deliberate among themselves. The process was open to the wider public with contributions streamed and the recommendations and rationales published. The eventual referendum result reflected the assembly conclusions far more closely than the opinion polls.

These kinds of deliberations are especially well suited to topics which require us to think through the needs and circumstances of different groups, to reflect on our own experiences but also to step outside them to think about what our whole society needs. They allow us to consider opposing arguments and reflect on judgements which are often finely balanced, providing the space and time to see through rhetoric and consider all sides of a question.

Another recent example is the project carried out by the Fabian Society, focused on the future of working-age benefits, involving expert consultation (including experts with direct experience of the social security system), a citizens' jury and a traditional survey (Abey & Harrop 2021). The project suggested that there is space for a new consensus to be forged around social security. Crucially, it engaged directly with the issue of what cost the participants were prepared to pay for a stronger social security system as well as what they felt was appropriate for different groups of benefit recipients. It found that there was support for incremental improvements, including more generous benefits for families with children, carers, disabled people and parents caring for young children; equalizing benefits for the under-25s; and better financial support for childcare. A more wholesale reform of the system, with levels of support matching the much higher levels of Loughborough University's minimum income standard, was seen as attractive but rejected because of its cost.

In the coming year we will emerge from the Covid-19 pandemic and reflect on 80 years of our welfare state, at the end of a decade of cuts which have severely undermined parts of it and amid rising public support for the system. The time is ripe for a larger-scale programme of deliberation to engage the public and those with the most direct experience of the system in shaping what the next 80 years should look like. I hope we can develop public consent for the principle that in a civilized, compassionate and just society we will not accept anyone's standard of living falling below a certain level. The level at which we are collectively willing to support one another, regardless of our actions, will be hotly contested. It might be destitution, or the poverty line, or (much more unlikely) the minimum income standard. But that is the debate that needs to happen and to be crafted with as much care as the similarly emotive issues of same-sex marriage and abortion in Ireland.

9

Public services for the digital age

So far, I've been talking about the type and level of financial support that's on offer in our social security system. But when you talk to people living in poverty, it's clear that it is equally important to consider non-financial support and how people are treated when they access both financial and non-financial services. An abstract view of poverty tends to focus purely on amounts of money and modelling behavioural responses to taxes, benefits, the labour market and so on. But the experience of poverty is as much about feeling powerless, dismissed and despised as it is about material hardship.

Public services – social security, employment support and health, social and local authority services – can build people up or knock them down. They can be a forum within which people are treated with dignity, listened to and respected, and where they are empowered to change their circumstances and realize their ambitions. Or they can be a place where people are made to feel they are problems to be fixed and are further disempowered and infantilized.

Before Beveridge and the reforms of the 1940s onwards, our public services were made up of a patchwork of voluntary and mutual organizations, Church provision and some limited local government funding and services. The Elizabethan Poor Law, introduced at the end of the sixteenth century, provided a legal underpinning and baked in the distinction between the deserving and undeserving poor. It ensured that the evolving system included detailed assessments and harsh conditions to prevent those classified as undeserving from receiving help that might encourage idleness and immorality. There were basically three roles available within this system: wise benefactor, passive supplicant and roguish malefactor. There were some positives to this system, particularly its localized nature and close involvement of what we would now call grassroots voluntary and community sector organizations. However, it failed to protect many people from hardship or provide the help that would enable them to build a better life for themselves. It was also wholly unsuited to the new industrial age.

The development of the industrial economy transformed all parts of society. Workers were collected in large numbers in cities, working in factories and on production lines and living in close proximity to the elites and middle classes. The growth of city slums gave rise to fears of disease spreading not only through the new working classes but also to the middle classes. The appalling living and working conditions were also thought to breed immorality and to weaken the strength of soldiers needed to fight first the Boer War and then the First and Second World Wars. New thinking also emerged about the causes of these ills, particularly unemployment. In Beveridge's first report on employment in 1909 he argued that unemployment was not only caused by individual laziness but was generated by the wider structures of the new industrial economy. It was a problem that would not be solved by local, individually focused solutions. It was an industrial problem that required an industrial solution.

From this kernel – published a year after the first Ford car came off the production line – emerged the shape of our modern public services. The ability to deliver standardized solutions at scale was the central requirement. Employment services needed to connect millions of workers to jobs in the new industries. Public health services needed to halt the spread of contagious diseases through mass immunization and quickly treat the victims of industrial accidents. Education services had to equip the workers of the future with the skills required by a wide range of large-scale employers. In the 1980s, this model was tweaked to introduce market mechanisms and non-state providers of services, aiming to cut costs and increase efficiency. But the basic approach has remained remarkably consistent even into the most recent reforms.

Reading Lord Freud's account of creating the new approach to employment support (the Work Programme) and the universal credit system, it is striking to see how this industrial mindset remained at the heart of the endeavour (Freud 2021). His approach assumed that the Jobcentre Plus network would handle the "standard volume business" of claimants who did not have significant barriers to work, whereas the "harder to help" would be put onto programmes contracted out to the private and voluntary sectors. When launching the report, both Tony Blair and Gordon Brown emphasized the role of the voluntary sector in these contracted-out services. In practice, however, Freud was clear from the start that the contracted-out parts of the system would be dominated by big corporates like Serco. The financial underpinning of the model required it. The whole point of contracting out services was to shift the upfront investment and risk to the contractors, with the government paying them later out of benefit savings generated by their success in getting people into work.

Beveridge worried that the system he was creating shut the voluntary sector out of the new services and put citizens and communities into powerless roles. Blair, Brown and Cameron all emphasized their desire for smaller voluntary and charity sector organizations to play more of a role. The mantra of "personalization" still echoes across public services from Jobcentres to healthcare. But none of this really changed the structure and approach of the systems created under the glow of the Fordist production line. The experience of many people is of systems that treat them as widgets: fitting them into the right box, applying the prescribed solution to fix them and moving them off the production line as the next widget hoves into view.

This model of public services has achieved mighty things. Our health services are highly successful at preventing illness through immunizations and at treating acute illnesses and injuries. Our education system has largely created a literate, numerate workforce and includes world-class higher education and research facilities. The Jobcentre Plus network and various incarnations of employment services have executed a work first approach efficiently, moving most people back into a job pretty speedily (even if it's a crappy job that doesn't pay much or last too long). It is increasingly clear, however, that our public services are not designed to solve the problems of our modern age or suited to the expectations of people growing up in a digital society.

In his book *End State*, James Plunkett (2021) recalls observing a meeting in 2008 between Gordon Brown and Tim Berners-Lee, the inventor of the internet. He describes seeing a gulf between Brown's language and conception of the government as a "'big clunking fist'... powerful but distinctively technocratic in its methods. What levers could we pull?" and Berners-Lee's talk of "platforms, standards and networks". Brown's thinking continued the industrial tradition, whereas Berners-Lee saw the world through digital eyes. The social reformer Hilary Cottam makes a similar argument, showing through her research and real-life experimental services how out of step old-style industrial services are with a world of networks, relationships, customization and consumer power. Cottam is part of a new generation of social reformers, pioneering a shift from industrial public services to relational ones. Along with Cottam and other independent thinkers, this shift is emerging from the work of voluntary and charity groups and local government leaders such as those engaged in the New Local organization.

Before we talk about the drivers and catalysts for this movement, let's take a couple of examples of what is meant by new relational services.

In her book *Radical Help*, Cottam (2018) describes five experiments through which she develops the ideas underpinning the new brand of services. In Swindon, Cottam and her team focused on services for families wrestling with multiple challenges, from trauma to addiction and violence. The families she meets have had years of "support" from social services and others. Cottam's team document the role of professionals from 20 different departments, all trying to manage or fix different aspects of what these families experience, do or refuse to do. The essence of the experiment was to agree that all these front-line workers would "step back". Instead, power and resources would be put in the hands of the families themselves and they would work out how to solve their problems. To help them, the families and Cottam's team jointly recruited a small group of people who would work with them. In contrast to the way that the professional services had been working, these relational workers would spend the majority of their time "by the side of the families" rather than wrangling the various systems and processes, and power would shift: "the families would drive and lead the change".

Later on, the book describes experiments in youth work, employment, healthcare and independent living for older people. There were common ingredients to all these: start by listening to the people the service wants to help, understand their experience and what they want to achieve; ask service users to identify solutions and draw on peer networks to support and share learning; put real power in the hands of service users; and prioritize relationships over processes. In each case, the existence and success of the experiment depended on local political and agency leaders being willing to sanction (and mandate if needed) the "stepping back" of the usual service providers and the shift of power to families and individuals.

In their report, "The Community Paradigm" (Lent & Studdert 2021), New Local provides more examples of this kind of approach to public services. One that is often cited is that of the Wigan deal, put together by Donna Hall (then the council chief executive) and Peter Smith (the council leader). Cambridgeshire council is another that has tried out the community approach to services at a local level. They stepped back from the usual hierarchies and institutions of service provision and redesigned services such as social care and economic development as a partnership between the council and the local community. The essence of the partnership was for assets such as buildings and budgets to be handed over to the community and for statutory services to be, as Cottam describes it, "reconfigured around relationships within and between communities" (Cottam 2021). The New Local report explains that:

> In practice, that means relocating council staff into the area, developing open conversations with service users and the community about what changes they would like to see in their lives, and working together to deliver those. This has the potential to be a far more collaborative relationship than those which characterized previous paradigms. Crucially, the priorities for the design and delivery of the services would be set with the community rather than by council officers or elected representatives.

The report goes on to explain in more detail how exactly services look different:

> The council has established training for frontline workers, particularly in the social care field, which draws on ethnographic techniques. These emphasize listening on behalf of the public servant, allowing the service user to take the lead and set the agenda, thereby avoiding the interaction

being shaped by preconceptions or bias ... Like increasing numbers of councils, Wigan also employs family group conferencing, which uses the power of family, friendship and community networks to support families in trouble and children at risk. This requires a very different role for social workers, based on facilitating network support and collaborating with that network, as opposed to imposing protection orders and care packages on children as a first resort.

So, what has been driving this movement towards community-driven, relational services? There has been a major shift in the nature and degree of social issues that our public services are required to respond to. Demographic changes are fuelling demand: longer lives and better medicine means that the major public health challenges are no longer infectious diseases (pandemics excepting) and child deaths but the growing number of people living with multiple long-term conditions. "Lifestyle-related" diseases such as type 2 diabetes and mental health conditions like depression and anxiety form an ever-increasing proportion of demands on health services. The prevention and management of long-term conditions is now the central mission of our health services, and they're just not designed for it. Funding and service provision is still geared towards clinical and hospital-based treatment for individual conditions. But the complexity of demand is rising, with people facing multiple challenges in their personal lives and communities. Inequality and poverty drive many social and health issues. In Wigan, rising demand and shrinking budgets led Donna Hall and Peter Smith to conclude that it simply wasn't possible to continue with "business as usual".

Our skills and education systems are good at delivering primary and secondary education and traditional academic qualifications but rubbish at enabling adults to retrain and update their skills to match the changing nature of jobs. Our employment services are good at pushing people quickly into jobs and bad at helping them to find high-quality work or progress upwards from badly paid jobs.

The model of large-scale generic services fails many of the groups who should be top priorities. Research with lone parents in Scotland (Yaqoob & Shahnaz 2021) recently found that the mainstream services on offer weren't designed to meet their needs, making them inaccessible. Specialist programmes with a better record are "rare and largely short-lived and/or delivered directly by under-funded third sector partners".

A major study from the Centre for Social Justice think tank focusing on the commissioning of disability services (Centre for Social Justice 2020) found a similar pattern. They describe an "oligopoly of [six] large, multinational providers" dominating the market for disability employment support. Smaller, voluntary and community sector organizations are effectively shut out of this market by the DWP's approach to contracting, despite them often having a better understanding of the needs of the individuals being supported and the local connections to go beyond trying to "treat" or "fix" one aspect of someone's life. The report describes a pilot in Greater Manchester taking a different approach. In the Working Well pilot, support for one set of disabled people was devolved to a partnership of local authorities and other local organizations. They were able to create more targeted and flexible services, to pool budgets and to integrate services across skills, mental health and employment for a single programme of support rather than service users bouncing from one service to another, each with their own targets and criteria.

This brings us to the fundamental challenge: how do we create this kind of change at scale? The shift needs to take place across the whole country, through myriad services, and it will take time, resources and energy. So how do we go beyond local experiments dependent on visionary individual leaders to sustain them? How do we protect the green shoots of change from being trampled by successive waves of short-term political imperatives? In short, how do we create change on an "industrial scale" if we can't use industrial methods?

First, we should build the principle of co-design into all public services. It should be expected and demanded that all services are developed and assessed by a team including people with direct experience of the issues and services under discussion. This doesn't mean doing a bit of qualitative research or testing the wording of a letter with a few claimants. It means putting together a team of people with different kinds of expertise – drawn from professional and personal experience – who work together on an equal basis. This sounds simple but it isn't. You can't just take the existing structures, processes and timelines and plonk a few experts by experience down in the middle of them. You have to redesign the processes, extend the timelines and work with people to define the scope of the project. It feels like a massive stretch to move from the existing model of public service design and delivery towards this approach and is reminiscent of the battle (still ongoing) to wrench government into the digital age.

To have any chance of making this happen requires bold leadership from the top of government. When the Scottish government set up Social Security Scotland, the minister in charge put values at the heart of the endeavour. Treating customers and staff with dignity and respect was at the core of design, recruitment and management. Beginning by listening to users, acting on their feedback and reporting back to them what had been done and why some ideas couldn't be taken up was vital. And this approach was embedded in the organization by the establishment of Experience Panels, so that the views of people who had experience of relevant panels were incorporated into each aspect of the work.

Once we have the leadership, we should set up a new Government Co-design Service. In 2011, the government announced the creation of the Government Digital Service. It was based on

a review by Martha Lane Fox recommending the body be created with "absolute control of the overall user experience across
digital channels" and run by a "CEO for digital". James Plunkett's
book details the painful battles that ensued and some of the gains
and losses for the new service. It may not have been a silver bul-
let, but it was certainly an engine for significant change. So, let's
try setting up a Government Co-design Service. Run by co-design
experts, with high-level civil service and political support and a
mandate to work across government services. The service would
find aspects of public services that are ripe for rethinking and
build up a community of people within government who have the
capability and commitment to make co-design work.

   One likely candidate for this approach is the coming reform
of disability benefits and support. The government's own social
security advisers have recommended that the DWP move quickly
to create a step change in their approach to engagement (Social
Security Advisory Committee 2020). They argue that the department should co-produce and publish a clear methodology for
engagement, report transparently on that engagement and recruit
a large-scale panel of disabled people with experience of social
security to consult regularly (as in Scotland), and that Jobcentres
should set up local panels to do the same. Similarly, a report from
the Social Market Foundation (Oakley 2021) presents a damning
picture of the failings of the current system for disabled people
and sees the answer as being a process of policy development to
be carried out in partnership with disabled people and organizations representing them, which would work out the underlying
principles that the reforms should follow, how it would judge
success, the options to achieve it and the choice for a new system
and how to deliver it. One fear that some have about this kind of
process is that those involved will make demands that the politicians and civil servants simply cannot meet, particularly around
levels of benefits. However, Jeane Freeman, the former social security minister in the Scottish government, argues that this fear is

misplaced.[1] Her view is that the answer lies in establishing an honest and adult relationship with people who experience the system. Listening isn't enough, you have to follow through on your promises, return to say what you've done and, crucially, explain the trade-offs and why some requests could not be met.

Second, the model of contracting out services needs a radical shake-up. We should move to a presumption of devolving budgets and responsibility down to the local level and to an approach to contracting which prioritizes the experience and involvement of service users, nurturing relationships and connections within communities. Such an approach is likely to boost the involvement of smaller voluntary and community sector and specialist providers over large multinationals. That has the potential to create additional value and prevent future problems as community organizations increase trust and connections between people and empower communities to support each other and solve problems locally.

Third, this needs to come alongside a change to our approach to funding and devolution. Cottam (2021: 10) reports the frustration of many local leaders at the current approach to innovation and devolution:

> Tinkering feels inadequate and traditional projects do not seem the right way forward. In particular there is an increasing rejection of short term outside-led innovation projects. Several leaders described to me their frustration at constantly finding themselves chosen as pilots by London based teams who look at deprivation data and turn up announcing a small scale (50k) collaboration. There is a growing perception that such projects raise expectations locally only to leave little behind in terms of improved local

---

1 In conversation with the author in November 2021.

conditions or capability. Two leaders told me how they had recently asked such teams to look elsewhere.

Cottam highlights the importance of growing skills and capability in local areas, rather than offering time-limited centralized consultancy. She advocates for place-based funding, in the millions of pounds, over periods of five to ten years, linked to a vision and philosophy not to predetermined outputs.

New Local suggests one way this might be done: "identifying significant funding streams, top-slice them from across Whitehall departments and pool them locally in place-based budgets". These place-based budgets would come with incentives to collaborate directly with people and co-design services. Pooling such budgets across an area would help to tip services towards prevention since the savings from reducing acute issues would be felt in the same place as the decision to invest in prevention. They point to the example of Denmark where local authority spending accounts for around two-thirds of all public spending. More local-level decision-making and control would enable services to go beyond even co-design and use deliberative decision-making, involving local people in the setting of strategic direction and the terms on which trade-offs are made. Designing services locally also opens up much more scope for civil society organizations to play a full role and bring their expertise and connections to bear. Few charities or social enterprises have the capacity to engage fully with policy or service delivery at a national level, but there is a rich tapestry of such groups at a local level and strong relationships, which can be leveraged.

One of the challenges in moving towards this approach will be how to prevent a return to the pre-1948 situation. It would be highly damaging to revert to a patchwork of services riven with cracks through which people fall and offering wildly different levels of support dependent on where you happen to live. We need to establish some consensual minimum standards: the commitment we make to each regardless of where you happen to live. And we need to create much better systems of transparency and accountability which enable local people and service users to understand the trade-offs and decisions made by local leaders and to hold them to account. Alongside this, we need systems which gather and publish data and evidence from across the country to enable us to hold national leaders to account for the structures, norms and constraints they create.

Fundamentally, we have to stop treating people as either the supplicants of the pre-Beveridge approach or the standardized widgets of the industrial age. We have to treat people as adults. As citizens. As people with ideas, ethics and the capacity to support one another and to make tough decisions in the common good. Our public services are no longer fit for purpose. We need to remake them for the digital age and to address the problems we face now rather than those of a previous era. In Carlotta Perez's terms, we need to develop a new role for the state and a new "common sense" in order to emerge from disruption and unrest and into the "golden age" of this wave of technological and social development.

10

Reimagining work

Beveridge was clear that maintaining full employment was necessary to his plan. It was a good in itself but was also vital to make the welfare state affordable and ensure workers would only need their unemployment payments for short periods. All that is still true, but the problems we now face in our labour market have changed.

Mass unemployment, although not necessarily gone for ever, has ceased to be the big challenge facing us. After the Great Recession and before Covid-19, the employment rate recovered amazingly strongly, but more and more workers were still pulled into poverty. The big issues now are low pay, lack of progression, insecurity and underemployment. Our central concern should be the quality of work that those at the lower end of the labour market are able to get, not just how many people have a job. So how do we prevent workers getting stuck in low-quality jobs?

One answer is to improve their skills and qualifications so that individuals can compete more effectively for better work and move employer to increase their pay, security and treatment. That is certainly necessary. The majority of young people from disadvantaged backgrounds reach the age of 16 without the baseline of five good GCSEs or their equivalent. The gap in attainment between children from richer and poorer families has remained stubbornly large and the Covid-19 pandemic wiped out a decade's worth of (very modest) progress in narrowing it (Education Endowment Foundation 2021). Five million adults lack basic reading, writing and numeracy skills. Accessing the next stages of education and getting a decent start in your working life is incredibly difficult without these basics.

Once adults are in the labour market, those with low levels of qualifications are far less likely to then get further training from employers than those who already have higher qualifications. The payback for doing training as an adult, in terms of getting better work or higher pay, is uncertain and very variable depending on the qualification, sector and where in the country you are. The barriers to low-paid workers getting more qualifications without the support of their employers are high; many people experience difficulties with finding the time to study when also working and caring, avoiding falling foul of benefit conditions or facing unacceptable hardship or debt if they try to reduce current work to allow training. They also face emotional uncertainty over what to do and whether it will all be worth it. Our skills system is especially unsatisfactory for workers who already have a level-two qualification of some kind (equivalent to GCSE level) but need something else to access better-quality work. Further education has been starved of funds and plagued by poor quality. We have some excellent higher education institutions, but the returns even to degrees from other parts of the system can be deeply unimpressive.

We need to radically improve the education and skills system for both children and adults. But concentrating on the skills and qualifications of individual workers is not going to solve the problem of poor-quality work or ensure that workers enjoy more of the benefits of growth. To solve this, we need to find ways to rebalance power in the labour market to enable more workers to demand better pay and conditions. As with public services, this rebalancing needs to go with the grain of a flexible, digital world rather than harking back to the industrial era.

A word about productivity. It is well known that the UK has a productivity problem, with historically low productivity growth since the 2008 financial crisis. Our productivity is especially poor in major service sectors like retail and hospitality, where our performance is significantly worse than in those same sectors in other countries (Innes 2018). Improving productivity overall and in those sectors is important for our economy and also helps to create more room for higher wages and enable greater progress for a given level of pressure. But it isn't enough. Rises in productivity don't always result in strong wage growth, particularly not in sectors dominated by low pay (Brocek 2019). Automation is likely to create more jobs than it destroys, but the jobs at most risk of disappearing are lower-paid ones done by people with fewer qualifications and less power to command higher wages elsewhere. The march of progress is therefore likely to erode their power even more. And there is a geography to this: parts of the country have local economies that are dominated by low-paid, low-skill jobs and where even those with mid-level qualifications struggle to find decent work.

As well as improvements to education and skills provision, we also need productivity strategies focused on sectors with lots of low-paid workers (especially retail and hospitality), boosting management skills, use of technology and reducing the use of temporary workers. To start changing the geography of opportunity, we need local industrial strategies that focus on creating inclusive growth that creates not just more jobs but better ones and raises the living standards of those most in need of it in each place. Harness the collective hiring, training and purchasing power of local institutions. Get local infrastructure like buses right. Target local growth plans and business support for sectors and businesses that deliver high-quality jobs with skills programmes to match (Hawking 2019).

But none of that will significantly change the power dynamics in our labour market, which will be vital to ensure that more vibrant local economies and more productive industries translate into better wages and conditions for workers.

State regulation clearly has an important part to play. The introduction of the minimum wage in 1999 was a landmark moment. Years later, George Osborne can be proud of his decision to raise it significantly and place it on the path to being set at two-thirds of the average wage. So can the many activists and the Living Wage Commission, whose unrelenting drive to sign up employers to the higher voluntary living wage has improved the lives of many workers directly and played a big part in laying the groundwork for a higher mandatory minimum wage. But, as we've seen, high hourly wages alone won't solve in-work poverty.

Stronger regulation to improve security at work and the rights of those at the bottom end is clearly required. The left and right of politics have traditionally been at loggerheads when it comes to regulation. But these days it is striking how much shared space there is. Nick Denys was head of policy for the Conservative Workers and Trade Unionists, founded by Conservative MP Robert Halfon, and is now policy adviser on employment and company law for the Law Society. He has long advocated strengthening employment law and enforcement. His priorities overlap with much of what is advocated by the TUC and others campaigning for better protection for workers, and with the widely supported recommendations of the Taylor Review of modern working practices (Taylor 2016).

The starting point is for the government to set out clear definitions of what the current murky employment statuses mean in terms of workers' rights and employers' obligations. Alongside that we should require that all individuals get a written statement telling them if they're a worker, an employee or self-employed, what their rights are and who their employer is.

Second is establishing stronger rights to tackle insecurity at the bottom end of the labour market. The Joseph Rowntree

Foundation, in collaboration with workers in poverty, has set out what a long-promised employment bill should focus on to boost the quality of work: the right to a secure contract that reflects your working hours, four weeks' notice of schedules and compensation for the last-minute cancellation of shifts (Schmuecker 2021). These are basic standards which would stamp out some of the worst practices and give a fairer playing field to those employers already treating workers with greater respect.

None of this is likely to make much difference, however, without much better enforcement of those rights than the current system offers. As Denys wrote in a report for the think tank the Centre for Policy Studies, "[t]he current British employment legislative framework puts the onus on the individual to assert that they are being exploited ... It does not undertake reviews of workplaces in the way that, for example, health and safety officers undertake reviews of places where food is prepared" (Denys *et al.* 2018).

The responsibility for enforcing workers' rights is split between four organizations: Her Majesty's Revenue and Customs (the tax department) for minimum wage, Employment Agency Standards Inspectorate, the Gangmaster and Labour Abuse Authority and the Health and Safety Executive. A new position of "director of labour market enforcement" was created in 2016, with the responsibility of producing a single strategy that covers the work of three of these bodies (excluding the Health and Safety Executive). However, the post is only for one or two days a week and has been both vacant and mired in controversy since the departure of Matthew Taylor in February 2021. Nick Denys and the Law Society, along with myriad others, believe that what is needed is a single enforcement body with the power to conduct proactive inquiries into sectors to find and address systemic issues, similar to the "market studies tool" used by the Competition and Markets Authority to investigate consumer rights.

The new body needs to be resourced sufficiently to take on the scale of abuse that exists. In 2015, a study by Citizens Advice found that one in ten people may be mislabelled as self-employed (Citizens Advice 2015). In 2020, the Low Pay Commission found that around 420,000 workers were paid less than the statutory minimum wage (Low Pay Commission 2020). The TUC has found that the UK's system falls far short of the International Labour Organization's (ILO) benchmark for the number of inspectors needed to enforce workers' rights effectively. The ILO recommends that countries have one labour market inspector per 10,000 workers. To meet that standard, the UK would need 3,287 inspectors; there are currently 1,490 (TUC 2021).

As well as stronger regulation, rights and enforcement, better social security will help, giving workers greater confidence to take risks and move jobs without the fear of being plunged into destitution if it doesn't work out. But regulation can't be the whole answer. Work, like other areas of life, is fundamentally about relationships and the complex interplay of different currents influencing individual day-to-day decisions by managers and workers. We need to look beyond the superficial simplicity of state intervention and think about how technology and innovation can offer new opportunities for workers to exercise power.

Many of you will have read the preceding pages while shouting "Unions! Why hasn't she mentioned unions? They're all about worker power for goodness sake!" The rise of unions and formal worker representation was, of course, an important factor shaping the postwar construction of the welfare state, the economy and our political system. Looking at today's labour market, the parts of it with the most low-paid and insecure jobs are where there is the weakest formal representation. In 1979, more than 13 million workers were part of unions; by 2019 it was 6.5 million, only about a quarter of employees (Department for Business, Energy and Industrial Strategy 2020). People with higher qualifications are twice as likely to be trade union members than those with no qualifications, reinforcing the power of those who already have more ability to bargain for higher pay or better conditions. Union members are highly concentrated in the public sector, where around half of employees are in unions, compared to only about one in seven private sector employees. On current trends, union membership is likely to keep falling as older union members retire while younger workers aren't signing up (Kelly & Tomlinson 2018). Changes to regulations, such as ensuring businesses allow unions to advertise their services in the workplace, would undoubtedly help but are unlikely to be enough to change the long-term trend away from unions in the private sector.

Kelly and Tomlinson's report highlights examples of some UK unions reaching out into low-pay parts of the economy and finding new ways to organize, including among self-employed workers who have been largely unrepresented in this country. They show that in the USA these efforts have gone much further and faster, particularly in their innovative use of new digital plat-forms to organize: from Coworker.org achieving paid parental leave at Netflix to platforms developed specifically for "Turkers", people working through Amazon's Mechanical Turk site which offers "micro-task work in return for micro-payments". As well as platforms to organize, there are also those focused on enabling workers to share and access information about pay and conditions across different employers. These have the scope to equip workers to make choices between sources of gig, agency or micro-work, rewarding good employer practices and punishing bad ones, as well as providing the basis for more organized campaigns.

These scattered examples have given rise to the realization that we need a more supportive infrastructure for what Gavin Kelly calls "pro-labour innovation". He argues that we need more formal and well-resourced places for such ideas to be incubated, for analysts thinking about how tech is transforming work to link up with people advocating for workers and for both to con-nect with sources of social investment for new ventures. This led him to establish Workertech – the "UK's first major innovation

partnership focused on using new technologies to improve workers' pay, prospects and power" – with backing from the Resolution
Foundation, the Joseph Rowntree Foundation, the Friends Provi-
dent Foundation, Accenture, the Ufi VocTech Trust and Trust
for London. The partnership opened with £1.3 million towards
the end of 2020; a good start, but a drop in the ocean compared
with what is required to harness digital technologies to empower
workers rather than exploit them.

Kelly argues that there is a gap in all of these mechanisms:
something to accelerate the establishment of better standards
in sectors with lots of poor practice and low union penetration,
on issues where employment law is too blunt to be a suitable
tool. Some progress can be made through the growing attention
of investors to "environmental, social and governance" issues.
Investors are certainly increasingly engaged in this, with growing evidence that good practice in these areas is linked to better
business performance. But there is currently much more understanding and activity in relation to the environmental part rather
than the social part, which should include a focus on workers'
rights and well-being. There is also a role for business support and
influencing HR professionals to advocate for better treatment of
workers. But Kelly argues that this will not go far or fast enough.
He believes we also need some modern version of wage councils:
sectoral bodies, with state backing but not under state control,
which set standards for their part of the economy.

The Welsh government is looking at using these to raise
conditions, starting with social care. In Scotland the Fair Work
Convention body, which advises the government, is developing
emerging sectoral deals. At the UK level, the then interim director of labour market enforcement, Matthew Taylor, pushed for
a licensing approach to sectors with significant levels of forced
labour such as car washes (before a not terribly amicable part-
ing of the ways with the Johnson government in 2021). In Kelly's
words, "without some version of [wage councils] the likes of the

Joseph Rowntree Foundation and Resolution Foundation will spend the next few decades banging on about decent work in the likes of care and hospitality but nothing much will change".[1]

The final way in which we can rebalance labour markets to empower workers and create better-quality work is by looking at the nature of businesses themselves. Research has looked at the range of business models within various sectors and particularly the extent to which they have relied on temporary, short-term workers to manage fluctuating demand or invested in a core of permanent staff. It found that both models existed within the same markets, facing the same pressures, and that both could succeed. The main factor determining which one an individual business adopted seemed to be the beliefs of the founder or leader of the company (Goulden 2010). We might think of this as the "Timpson vs Ashley" paradigm.

James Timpson has become the poster boy for ethical business, putting kindness and trust at the heart of his company's culture, and investing in training and staff welfare as well as more targeted measures like employing ex-offenders. As he wrote in the *Sunday Times* in 2019:

> I have worked out how to survive the retail storm: invest more in looking after our people. It may seem mad to some, but the more we care for our colleagues, the better the Timpson key-cutting and shoe-repair business seems to perform. Over the past five years, we have opened 1,000 new shops, sales and profits have doubled – and we still have cash in the bank. Next year, we will spend a further £8m looking after our colleagues. It's the best money we can spend.

---

1 Gavin Kelly, correspondence with the author, August 2021.

Mike Ashley's success, on the other hand, was built on an agency worker model and involved shocking levels of exploitation. A 2016 report by MPs found that workers were paid below the minimum wage and penalized for taking short breaks to drink water and taking time off sick. Ashley claimed to be unaware of all this, but MPs were frankly sceptical: "It therefore seems incredible to us that the owner, whose name is inextricably linked with the brand of Sports Direct, and who visits the warehouse at least once a week, would have no idea of the working conditions and practices there, when they have been highlighted in the media and in Parliament since 2015" (Business, Innovation and Skills Committee 2016). Put simply, we need to tilt the structures and incentives in our economy to nurture and grow the pool of Timpsons and shrink the influence of the Ashleys.

We can achieve this through many means: changing regulations to reduce the competitive dividend from exploitative business models; growing the space for ethical leaders through investor and consumer action; and using procurement and business support to nurture and reward better approaches and social value.

One idea that has gained increasing currency in recent years is the idea that more "purpose-driven" businesses could help to rebalance our labour market, increasing the range of choices on offer to both workers and consumers. The challenge is that this will only make a significant dent on the issue of poverty if there is an enormous increase in the proportion of such businesses in the economy. At the current level it is hard to see purpose-driven businesses transforming the lives of millions of workers. But it is worth trying to grow this part of the economy, even if that's unlikely to be a substitute for the changes to regulation and enforcement set out above.

The UK's co-operative movement has roots back to the nineteenth century and before, with the Rochdale Pioneers established in 1844 evolving into the modern Co-operative Group.

Today, there are just over 7,000 Co-ops in the UK, with a combined turnover of £39.7 billion (Co-operatives UK 2021). In recent years, "platform co-ops" have developed: digital platforms that provide a service or sell a product and are collectively owned or governed by the people who participate in it. These are positioned as alternatives to the big tech platforms, such as Amazon and Uber, which have tilted power away from workers and pushed pay and conditions down. There are only a few platform co-ops in the UK so far, and very few that have come out of the start-up phase to become established businesses. Work by Nesta and Co-operatives UK (Borkin 2019) has identified a range of ways to grow the sector, most importantly proposing a platform co-op fund to provide the capital investment that is required since other sources are hard to tap into for these fledging co-ops.

Co-ops focus on ownership and control, tilting both towards members, consumers or workers. "Purpose-driven businesses" can have different forms but are defined by being run for profit (unlike social enterprises) but driven by a mission to solve "the problems of people and planet", as Profession Colin Mayer put it in a World Economic Forum article (Mayer 2020). Ed Boyd (formerly a special adviser in the Cameron government) set up the ReGenerate think tank to work out how to accelerate the growth of purpose-driven businesses. They have demonstrated the case for more purpose-driven businesses in terms of appetite among business leaders, public support and achieving business success and sustainability. The positive impacts of purpose-driven businesses can be seen in businesses that improve people's lives, achieve environmental goals and attract, retain and make the most of their workers.

There is no real estimate of how many purpose-driven businesses there are in the UK. One leading organization is B Lab, which grows the "B Corp" movement of businesses (currently 300) who have met their high standards of "social and environmental performance, public transparency, and legal accountability to balance profit and purpose". Clearly, to make changes to the UK's labour market at scale, these types of business models will need to take hold far more widely than is currently the case. ReGenerate has looked at some ways of enabling this, showing that companies are held back from being purpose driven and that it is too hard for their investors and other stakeholders to judge and reward or punish their impact. They have proposed: changes to our legal framework to make it easier for a company to be registered and run as purpose driven; action on impact standards so that investors and consumers can judge a company's impact more easily; and the provision of more resources and support to help businesses become purpose driven and entrepreneurs set up new purpose-driven companies.

This shift could be helped by changes to the regulations governing companies, for instance requiring them to pay heed to the interests of all their stakeholders rather than shareholders alone. Company law currently directs incorporated companies to focus on shareholder value, "while having due regard for other stakeholders". That means a business can be purpose driven if that purpose is totally at one with the interests of shareholders. But where shareholders are demanding short-term profits, it is risky for company directors to take actions that might be in the longer-term interests of the purpose of the company, or to do things for the benefit of other stakeholders, if it would conflict with the short-term profit motive.

It is hard to know how much difference such changes to company law would make. As Nick Denys argues, fundamentally, companies are owned by shareholders and their interests will always trump those of other stakeholders unless the shareholders themselves choose otherwise. However, I think there is potential for changes at scale, particularly if more investors decide to prioritize these issues; ReGenerate finds that ESG (environmental, social and governance) funds are set to outnumber conventional funds by 2025.

Accelerating the growth of purpose-driven companies, co-ops and the like would not magically raise wages or improve job security. But it could start to change the norms and assumptions governing our economy. Proponents hope to move away from the philosophy of the Chicago School of Business and Milton Friedman, which became dominant in the 1980s and put pure profit motives and returns to shareholders at the forefront of business thinking. The new approach would still see profit as a vital goal of business, but it would not be the only goal. This could open up space for more businesses to adopt practices which support environmental and social goods as well as profits. It would enable more ethically minded entrepreneurs to thrive, which could change the landscape of job options for workers currently stuck in low-paid, unfulfilling jobs.

11

Managing modern markets

The combination of well-regulated market capitalism and active government redistribution have led to enormous rises in living standards and reductions in poverty over the last two centuries (Ortiz-Ospina 2017). Changes to how production was organized and the rise of industrialization led to an explosion of expertise, innovation and productivity (as well as the continued exploitation of people in many parts of the world which had been colonized or forced to feed the economic success of dominant powers). People in countries that embraced market capitalism are able to enjoy living standards, comforts and leisure unimagined by their predecessors and still far out of reach of vast swathes of the world's population. These gains were not simply the result of untrammelled markets however. They also rested on the growth of governmental ambition and reach. GDP has grown massively in the last century but, equally importantly, government spending as a share of national income has also shot up since the 1930s: from under 10 per cent in the UK at the start of the twentieth century to over 30 per cent by the end of the century (Brien & Keep 2018).

Ironically, given that their proponents tend to be locked in conflict, it seems to have been the combination of globalization and public spending, especially on social safety nets, that have delivered better living standards and lower poverty. We have talked a lot so far about the safety net side of this equation, but what about the markets side?

At the heart of market capitalism is the idea of the active consumer. The market organizes itself to meet the evolving needs of its consumers, competing for their custom and innovating to get an edge over the competition either by reducing prices or improving the goods or service being bought. Since poverty is about someone's resources not meeting their needs, reducing costs can free people from poverty if it means their resources can go further. When food prices are low, more people can feed themselves. If the cost of heating falls, more people can afford to keep their homes warm. Over a decade of research on living standards and the cost of meeting our basic needs, Loughborough University's minimum income standards programme has offered striking examples of the power of this to improve people's lives (Hirsch *et al.* 2018). In 2018, a laptop, broadband internet and smartphone cost less than the price of a landline telephone and pay-as-you-go mobile in 2008. The rise of technology reduced costs across other areas of life by enabling people to shop online and compare prices far more effectively than in the pre-digital period.

Traditionally, in market economies regulation needs to do two main things. First, it must ensure consumers can make well-informed choices and businesses can't get their competitive edge by falling below agreed standards of health and safety or exploiting their workers. Second, monopolies must be prevented where companies dominate such a big share of a market that they can inflate prices or cut standards without consumers being able to realistically shop around to find a better deal. When monopolies take hold, they don't only create higher prices, they also stifle innovation and improvements in goods or services. Consumers find themselves paying over the odds for shoddy products and bad customer service and entire sectors become fossilized and stuck at the level of development which suits the current big hitters. Businesses pour energy into lobbying to keep their privileged position and marketing to prevent consumers realizing they're being fleeced, instead of innovations which will disrupt the status quo.

In his book, *End State*, however, James Plunkett sets out a compelling critique of the way we regulate markets, showing how out of step they are with the challenges of a digital economy. Plunkett focuses on the firms he calls the "superstars", particularly the four big tech firms: Google, Facebook, Amazon and Apple. He cites 2017 research showing that the top 1 per cent of companies in the USA were "crushing" the rest. In 2018, McKinsey research looking at the world's 6,000 biggest firms found that the top 10 per cent captured 80 per cent of profits, and the top 1 per cent captured 36 per cent of profits. The middle 60 per cent of firms made practically no profit. This led to massively increased prices charged by firms at the top and a breakdown in usual patterns of competition.

The evidence that these firms now operate as harmful monopolies is found in a 2020 study of their profits. Plunkett explains that this study shows that Google is making a return on capital of about 40 per cent and Facebook of 38 per cent, compared to a return of 6 per cent for Tesco. Crucially, their high rates of return have lasted for several years, showing "entrenched market power", rather than being short-term spikes as you'd expect if usual market forces operated such that they reaped the rewards of innovation which were then reduced by the competition catching up, spurring the next round of innovation and thus benefiting consumers.

Current market regulation is obviously failing to address this, partly because it focuses on whether mergers or takeovers will give a single company too great a share of a specific market. But, as Plunkett explains, Google, Facebook and their ilk don't wait for competitors to get big enough to be a threat and then try to take them over; they buy start-ups and absorb their ideas, data and so on while they are still small. They also buy companies in totally different markets, acquiring technology or other capabilities that entrench their power. Neither of these approaches raises red flags in a regulatory system that looks only at their overall share of distinct markets but both extend their power and prevent healthy competition, raising costs and acting as a drag on innovation that would benefit consumers.

So how do we tackle these new-style monopolies? Plunkett reflects the insights of Professor Diane Coyle, one of the world's leading competition experts, in saying that the traditional approach of breaking up large companies is unlikely to work and would actively damage consumers. In a digital age we want seamless connections between different social media accounts and apps. We want to use a single search engine, not search on several to be sure we've covered all the bases. We want our online lives to be simpler, not more complicated. He also argues that breaking the big tech giants up wouldn't work as they would find ways to structure themselves to avoid a break-up and others could just use the same tactics to grow again. Instead, Plunkett advocates a new approach for the digital age: "if we want to harness the world's technology giants for public good, we shouldn't break them up – we should open them up" (Plunkett 2021).

So how would this work? As is so often the case in this new digital age, data and networks are the central points to focus on. Big tech firms have access to enormous amounts of data which they use to tailor their products and services and how they sell them. The more successful a company becomes the more data it has, which it uses to cement its position at the top while crushing smaller fish. They can also exploit network effects: the more people who join a platform or network the more attractive it is and the more people it attracts. Again, this reinforces the dominance of whoever controls the platform and of those who have privileged access to it.

Plunkett therefore suggests we stop thinking of these big tech giants as market monopolies that should be broken up and to start thinking of them as "natural monopolies and public assets

... a digital platform of strategic social value". The goal of regulation should become the creation and maintenance of access to the power of these platforms and of the data they generate. This data is the new engine of innovation, so we need to open it up to other companies and researchers, to harness it as a public good to drive innovation which benefits consumers instead of a private hoard which enables a few companies to exploit consumers and stifle the competition.

Plunkett's second idea is to "harmonize the technical standards that keep these ecosystems separate". We should create a set of standards which tech firms are required to use and which ensure that other businesses can integrate into the big platforms freely, just as we require all USB ports to be compatible so we can choose between products instead of only being able to plug a Dell memory stick into a Dell computer. This would push the power back to consumers, enabling us to move our data between platforms, to cross-post between social media and invite friends on one to join us on another. Plunkett points out that this would make our lives as consumers simpler rather than more complicated and drive innovation by enabling developers to build things that work across different tech ecosystems instead of being beholden to a platform controller for access.

The third idea advanced by Plunkett focuses on how we ensure consumers are charged fairly for the goods or services they buy. Anyone who regularly books hotel rooms around the country will be familiar with dynamic pricing: the price of the same hotel room in the same place can more than double if you book at a busy time. The same applies to almost everything else we buy online but it is often invisible to the average consumer. There are even services available to help people track this so they can identify the optimum time to buy something. For instance, dedicated vinyl buyers use the CamelCamelCamel website to understand price fluctuations on Amazon. But these kinds of services are still pretty niche and require more time, energy and know-how than many of us have.

Some of this dynamic price setting is fair enough: the last hotel room in Edinburgh during the annual festival is worth a lot more than the same hotel room in October when there are fewer tourists and more choice. The problem is that the prices we see when we search for something online don't just reflect the usual market factors of scarcity or quality. They are shaped by the characteristics of the person searching. If two people walk into a shop at the same time they will see the same products and be able to buy them at the same price. But two people can search for the same thing online and see different options depending on their previous purchasing history: for example, richer consumers are shown more expensive products. The digital marketplace has opened up much wider choices to many of us, but as it becomes more sophisticated, its design is now acting to reduce that choice, to hide some options and guide consumers towards the ones that will benefit the companies that control the digital shopfront. The regulator the Competition and Markets Authority has published detailed research (Competition and Markets Authority 2021) into the ways that algorithms and machine learning can reduce competition and harm consumers, often through personalization penalties.

Companies have more and more data about consumers which they use, through algorithms, to shape the options offered to each consumer, the order in which they appear and what prices they are offered. The Competition and Markets Authority research cites examples from Uber, casinos in Las Vegas, more pedestrian companies such as Staples and B&Q and whole industries such as insurance. The result is manipulation of costs in ways that disadvantage consumers in general and particular types of customers especially, such as older customers, those in some places or in some ethnic groups being offered higher prices and worse deals. One example is the cost of online SAT preparation services being higher in some parts of the USA than others, and people with "Asian names" being twice as likely to live in areas with higher prices than other consumers. In 2016, Amazon Prime expanded its same-day delivery service but excluded mainly Black neighbourhoods (Ingold & Soper 2016). Research by the Brookings Institution (Turner Lee *et al.* 2019) has documented examples such as algorithms in recruitment that disadvantage female job applicants and in online searches that offer adverts for high-interest credit cards to people with African American names. Algorithmic pricing can also lead to collusion between companies (deliberately or unconsciously), raising prices for consumers, for example when German petrol stations raised their margins after adopting algorithmic pricing because it reduced competition.

Where these new market practices reduce competition and raise prices, it becomes harder for those on low incomes to buy what they need. In many cases, this general effect is exacerbated by patterns which further disadvantage groups more likely to be in poverty: people from some ethnic minority groups, women and less active consumers.

The UK Competition and Markets Authority believes that the increasing use of algorithms for decision-making may be positive, arguing that "algorithms can be subject to greater and more in-depth scrutiny than human decision-makers". But it acknowledges that using consumer law to protect people from algorithmic discrimination is an "unexplored area" and is establishing a new Digital Markets Unit to get to grips with this challenge. Their report makes it clear that successful regulation in this new digital landscape will require the new unit to have the power to gather enough information to judge the impact of algorithmic systems, the skills and tools to monitor and carry out investigations and the development of new standards against which to judge companies. Both the UK's Competition and Markets Authority and the Brookings Institute recommend "regulatory sandboxes" in which companies can test algorithms and identify biases in their outcomes without falling foul of data protection and other regulations.

Plunkett gives a number of examples of failed attempts by regulators to use existing approaches to rebalance the scale between consumers and companies, particularly the ineffectiveness of trying to set detailed rules about how businesses should present information to encourage consumers to shop around. He advocates "principles-based regulation" as an alternative. Instead of regulators enforcing specific rules governing companies' behaviour they would focus on outcomes and judge companies on whether they are behaving in ways that achieve the right ones:

> In a rules-based system, it's the bureaucrat who holds the clipboard, wandering the factory while checking off a list; if they happen to tick the wrong box, they bear many of the costs themselves. In an outcome-based system, the onus shifts onto companies. Once they've seen the principles set by the regulator, they have to make their own boardroom judgements about whether they're crossing the line, risking fines if they get it wrong. (Plunkett 2021)

Thus, a company would have to ensure that women, for example, weren't systematically being charged higher prices than men or being offered lower-quality products. This approach has the potential to be a game changer for consumers, but it has so far proved challenging for regulators to enforce. Judging whether principles have been met is intrinsically more difficult, nuanced and feels riskier than ticking off a list of rules. As Martin Coppack, director of the Fair By Design campaign, remarks:

> Consumer organizations liked the [Financial Conduct Authority's] Treating Customers Fairly principles when they came out but are disillusioned now due to the minimum impact they have had. If principles-based regulation is brought in the supervision needs to be resourced and regulators have to deal with more nuance and uncertainty

in terms of enforcing. This requires new skill sets and more nerve when not relying on rules when disciplining firms.[1]

Now that the Financial Conduct Authority is introducing what has been positioned as a tougher Consumer Duty, the question is whether they will beef up their supervision and enforcement or if it will prove similarly disappointing.

So far, I've talked about broad ways in which consumer markets need to be rebalanced for the digital era. Achieving this would be beneficial for all of us and would help to tackle poverty by reducing costs and increasing innovation which can be particularly important for people on low incomes who have fewer options and are likely to have to go without essentials if the cost of living outstrips their resources. But this isn't enough. We also need measures which focus on the poor deal many low-income consumers get in specific markets.

Almost all low-income households pay a "poverty premium" which costs them on average £490 (Fair By Design 2021). People in poverty pay more for car insurance because they live in a deprived area, more for credit because they are deemed a higher risk and more for energy if they have a pre-payment meter or don't pay by direct debit. Research with people using the services of poverty charity Turn2Us found that they were spending the equivalent of 14 weeks of food shopping to access the same services as those who were better off.

Fair By Design was set up by the Joseph Rowntree Foundation, Big Society Capital and the Barrow Cadbury Trust. It includes a social investment fund to grow innovations to make markets fairer and a programme of policy and advocacy work to collaborate with regulators, government and businesses to "design out the poverty premium". It has produced two guides for regulators

---

1 In conversation with the author, November 2021.

and firms showing how to embed "inclusive design" in their product design and policy development; design that ensures products and services are accessible and useable by as many people as possible, with a particular eye on those groups most likely to be excluded without it. To loosen the grip of poverty, it's especially important for these to be adapted in markets for essentials – such as energy, credit and insurance – where people in poverty currently pay more and are pulled into greater hardship as a result. We are seeing progress, with the Competition and Markets Authority, Financial Conduct Authority and Ofgem having recognized the importance of inclusive design. But we need much greater action. Regulators across the board need to recognize that people on low incomes are being disadvantaged by the way consumer markets currently operate. They are less "valuable" customers, who are seen as higher risk, and are more likely to be in insecure jobs, have fluctuating health conditions and be digitally excluded. Every regulator should be proactively investigating the poverty premium in their areas and requiring action to achieve greater fairness and access for low-income consumers.

A final note about markets. It would be strange to write about the big challenges facing our society and not mention climate change and the challenge of reaching net zero in time to avoid even greater environmental damage. Climate change and poverty are intertwined, both globally and in the UK. People on low incomes contribute much less to causing climate change than those who are better off (Banks *et al.* 2014). They are less likely to have cars and use planes and they have lower consumption due to their lack of resources. However, they are at higher risk from many of the immediate impacts of climate change, disproportionately living in places likely to be flooded and less likely to have insurance to help them meet the resulting costs.

From a poverty perspective, there are things to be optimistic about, especially the opportunity to create green jobs and support people into new career paths which can be designed with progression opportunities, decent pay and security at their heart. But there are also serious concerns, particularly around the role of costs and taxes. Market mechanisms are likely to be vital tools in achieving net zero, flushing out the environmental cost of our current way of life and creating incentives for both firms and consumers to change their behaviour. However, there is a serious risk that necessary steps to address climate change could end up making poverty worse unless they are designed carefully.

A 2020 study by the London School of Economics examined the way in which a UK carbon tax could affect different groups (Burke *et al.* 2020). They modelled the impact of a carbon tax of £50 per tonne of carbon dioxide in 2020, rising to £75 in 2030. They found that it hit lower-income households much harder than wealthier ones by taking a bigger proportion of their income. However, this varied depending on the type of carbon tax: a carbon tax on energy fuels was regressive but one on transport was generally progressive (because better-off people spend more on transport than poorer ones). The researchers found that the negative impacts of carbon taxes could be counteracted if some of the money raised is used specifically to help low-income families, for instance by paying for energy efficiency measures which reduce emissions and also their energy costs.

A further challenge for the design of market mechanisms to achieve net zero, such as a carbon tax, is the need to think globally rather than just domestically. As the Centre for Policy Studies has shown (Lodge 2020), a carbon tax that only acknowledges the environmental cost of activities within our own borders creates perverse incentives and risks undermining its ultimate purpose. In 2019, the UK's "coal-free fortnight" turned out to have been achieved by importing Dutch electricity which probably came from coal-fired plants. Ideas such as a carbon border tax on imports will have to become part of our approach if we are to achieve genuine environmental benefits rather than just shuffling the cause of the climate crisis around between countries.

Well-regulated and efficient markets can improve the living standards of people on low incomes, as well as creating gains for consumers overall and generating the taxes which pay for our social security system and other public services. However, markets constantly evolve and regulation needs to keep up. We urgently need to update our approach to consumer markets for the digital global age. Now we are looking to the future with ever greater urgency to work out how to solve the climate crisis and shift to a sustainable economic model. We need to design an approach which avoids making people on low incomes inadvertent casualties of the race to reach net zero.

12

Tax, wealth and housing

Finally, it's time to talk about the twin elephants in the room. First, taxes: how we raise the money to pay for the public services we all rely on and which are crucial to slaying the poverty giant. Second, housing: housing costs are a central driver of poverty, locking people into poverty even as wages rise. Too many people in poverty are trapped in overcrowded, damp, unsafe homes. High costs and insecurity pull increasing numbers into homelessness. These two issues are linked. The structure of our tax system helps to shape both the housing and labour markets. How we raise money is as important as how much we raise and how we choose to spend it. Increasing the supply of housing is vital but not sufficient. We also need to change the structure of the housing market and the ways in which housing operates as an asset as well as a home.

In 2018, David Willetts (a Conservative MP and minister in the 1990s and again in the Coalition government from 2010 to 2014, now in the House of Lords, colloquially known as "Two Brains") gave a speech in which he delivered some home truths to his fellow boomers (Willetts 2018):

> We are the first generation to have lived our entire lives under the modern welfare state. We have benefited from Britain's house price boom which has made home

ownership unaffordable for our children. We have done so well compared with the younger generation in so many ways that we cannot just turn to them to pay for our health and social care. And it is this cost above all – paying for a service we particularly benefit from in our old age – which is pushing public spending inexorably upwards. We are going to have to make a contribution too. And when we look at how we should do this there is one obvious source – the wealth we are sitting on.

It doesn't require two brains to know that he was right, or that actually achieving this shift is a political nightmare. But the argument that regularly breaks out about wealth taxes and inheritance needs to be understood in the broader context of how both our tax system and the shape of our national wealth have changed over the last few decades, and the pressures which make it imperative that we grasp the nettle of redesigning our approach to both.

The usual summary of the British attitude to tax and spending is that we want European public services and US-level taxes. Otherwise known as the "I want to lose weight, but I also like cake" approach to public policy. In response to these contradictory demands, governments have tended to resort to stealthy, piecemeal approaches, tweaking the tax system and rolling back proposals that prove too controversial. This has left us with a tax system that is complicated, unbalanced and inadequate, riven with perverse incentives and a provider of ample employment for lawyers and accountants but nightmarish for the rest of us.

Looking at the big picture on tax, the UK ranks 23rd out of 37 countries in the OECD in the size of our tax take compared to GDP (OECD 2020). We raise more tax than the USA, New Zealand, Canada and a few other countries but less than most European countries. What is interesting is that the level of tax raised across most of the G7 countries has risen significantly since the 1960s, but the UK has had the smallest increase in the overall tax burden, with our tax take only rising from 30.1 per cent in 1965 to 33 per cent in 2017 (Tetlow & Marshall 2019) and staying pretty much completely flat since 2000. Even with the bumper tax rises announced by Rishi Sunak in 2021, the Office for Budget Responsibility expects this to rise to reach 36 per cent in 2026–7 (Office for Budget Responsibility 2021).

Three big taxes make up the vast majority of this: income tax, national insurance and value-added tax (VAT). Smaller amounts come from taxes on business (mainly corporation tax) and other consumption taxes (fuel duty, tobacco, alcohol, air travel). The major change that has happened in the UK tax system in recent decades is in the balance of these taxes. The balance has shifted away from taxing income and specific goods (like fuel, tobacco or alcohol) and towards national insurance and general consumption taxes (VAT). Analysis from the Institute for Government shows that, in 1975, 40 per cent of tax revenues came from taxing income, profits and capital gains (the profit made from selling something that has increased in value compared to when you bought it); 17.5 per cent came from social security and payroll taxes (national insurance contributions) and just under 9 per cent from broad consumption taxes (VAT). But by 2016, only 27 per cent of taxes came from income taxes paid by individuals (income tax, capital gains tax, etc.) with national insurance rising to 19 per cent and consumption taxes (VAT) to over 20 per cent. This trend continued in 2021, with a further increase in national insurance payments announced, to take effect in 2022.

We've already talked about the inexorable pressures on our public services and social security system, driven by our ageing population and changing healthcare needs. Our tax system is creaking under the weight of meeting these pressures and is also out of step with the shape of the modern economy. Modernizing it would allow us to raise more money, more efficiently and more fairly. There are three major challenges we need to face up to:

(1) we're terrible at taxing wealth, especially housing wealth; (2) we tax people who work for themselves much more lightly than employees; and (3) we're bad at taxing global corporations.

TAXING HOUSING WEALTH

In 1980, when The Police's "Don't Stand So Close to Me" topped the charts, the total wealth held by people in the UK amounted to about three times the national income. By 2020, as "Own It" spent three weeks at number one, enormous rises in wealth meant it was now seven times as high as our national income (Leslie & Shah 2021). Despite this massive increase in wealth, tax on it has stayed flat. This matters because wealth is even more unequally distributed than income and because we are missing out on sorely needed tax revenues, placing even more pressure on other taxes paid by working-age people and on spending cuts which hit that same group hardest.

The biggest driver of increasing wealth, particularly since the financial crisis in 2008, has been rises in the price of assets, mainly property. People have become wealthier primarily because they owned things which have become more valuable. They are passive beneficiaries not active wealth creators. The richest tenth of UK households hold more than half of all wealth. On average, someone in the wealthiest one per cent has £5 million in net wealth, more than 60 times that held by the average person (Leslie 2020). Wealthy people tend to be retired or close to retiring, both because of their age and because, as David Willetts pointed out, the baby boomer generation have benefited from very significant wealth gains over their lives. The Covid-19 pandemic has only increased this inequality. People who were already on low incomes and with little wealth have tended to lose income, run down their savings and end up in more debt. Those with higher incomes have been able to save more, with asset prices, especially housing, rising significantly during the pandemic and increasing their wealth further.

The nature of this growth in wealth, and the tax structure which has encouraged it, has compounded the dysfunction in the housing market which has trapped so many people in poor-quality, expensive and insecure homes.

"An Englishman's home is his castle". Leaving aside the myriad problems with this aphorism from a modern perspective, it captures something of the deep-seated desire to own your own home which is such a feature of the UK's culture and politics. But, as we've seen, home ownership rates peaked at the start of the 2000s and have fallen since, leaving more and more families renting their homes for longer and longer. But while fewer people are able to buy one home, more and more are buying multiple houses. This is mainly people buying additional houses to rent out and, to a lesser extent, second homes. Almost two million people own buy-to-let properties (Gangham 2019). Analysis by the Centre for Policy Studies in 2019 (Edwards 2015) found that nearly all the homes built between 2005 and 2015 were bought by private landlords. They highlight changes to the mortgage market after the 2008 financial crisis as central to the decrease in home ownership and the corresponding boom in the buy-to-let market.

The shift to buy-to-let was also indirectly fuelled by the introduction of Right to Buy. The policy succeeded in its intention to expand home ownership to people living in social housing who had never been able to afford to buy. However, about four in ten ex-council houses sold through Right to Buy ended up as part of the buy-to-let sector (Apps 2015). As we've seen, many private renters are stuck paying high rents, subsidized by housing benefit, because they can't get into lower-rent social homes or afford to buy a house. The failure to replace homes sold through Right to Buy depleted the stock of affordable rented homes for those on low incomes and cut off the route to home ownership that had been opened up for them.

The boom in multiple property ownership is concentrated among people who are rich in terms of income and other wealth.

Analysis by the Resolution Foundation found that two-thirds of buy-to-lets and more than half of second homes are owned by the richest fifth of households. They're bought to provide rental income, inheritance or as part of pension provision. This is going to increase inequality for future pensioners: richer people are more likely to own the home they live in rather than have to rent into older age, they're more likely to have a private pension and this research shows that those investing in property for later life tend to be doing so alongside saving through a pension, not instead of it.

Our tax system treats much of this mostly unearned wealth extraordinarily lightly. The enormous increase in wealth through the rising value of people's main homes is exempt from capital gains tax. Inheritance tax is hopelessly out of step with the rising value of bequests and the ever-increasing role of inheritance in entrenching inequality. Only 4 per cent of estates pay any inheritance tax at all. With around £127 billion passed on, the inheritance tax rate is effectively only 3.5 per cent (Corlett 2018). You can inherit £1 million and pay no tax on it at all. If you know you're going to have a lot of wealth to pass on you can avoid paying any tax on far more than this by doing so more than seven years before you die. That's particularly helpful for people with multiple properties or other forms of wealth that go beyond owning their family home. The unfairness is compounded by exemptions that are supposedly for family businesses and farms but actually made good use of by wealthy people with clever accountants rather than primarily helping small businesses or family farms.

Less than 1 in 20 people in the UK pay inheritance tax. But it is still extremely unpopular and seen as an unfair tax on giving, with an apparently high rate: the flat rate is 40 per cent, which sounds high if you're used to a 20 per cent income tax rate, even if the effective tax on inheritance is actually much lower than on income. The sense that it is avoidable by the really wealthy adds to the sense of unfairness. Attempts to reform it or to tap into more of the accumulated wealth of richer groups are torpedoed by labelling it a "death tax".

Council tax has the dubious honour of being the UK's only completely regressive tax (even taking account of the help provided to some of those on low incomes through Council Tax Support). Introduced in haste in 1993 as a temporary measure after the poll tax debacle, it still uses property values set in 1991 and falls most heavily on people with the lowest incomes. The Institute for Fiscal Studies finds that the poorest tenth of the population pay 8 per cent of income, the next 50 per cent pays 4 per cent or 5 per cent and the richest 40 per cent only 2–3 per cent (Bourquin & Waters 2019).

There have been some welcome policy tweaks in recent years focused on people owning additional properties, such as a Stamp Duty surcharge on buy-to-let properties in 2016 and the phasing out of mortgage interest tax relief by cutting it by a quarter each year from 2017 onwards. These do seem to be starting to reduce the propensity for individuals to leap into the buy-to-let market. But there has been little progress on the much bigger changes needed to bring our tax system into the modern era and tap into housing wealth more fairly.

We could make a good start by:

1.   Reforming capital gains tax so that it more closely matches income tax rates and removes incentives for people to characterize income as capital gains, as recommended by the Office for Tax Simplification (2020).

2.   Replacing inheritance tax with a "lifetime receipts tax" covering inheritances and gifts received over someone's life, learning from the experience of Ireland and France. It could be set up with an allowance that exempted most inheritances (since most people pass on relatively low amounts of wealth) and with a lower rate than 40 per cent and still raise much

more money than the currently system, more fairly and
efficiently (Corlett 2018).

3.   Replacing council tax with a progressive property tax and
one paid by owners rather than those renting a house. This
could be designed to tax additional properties and second
homes at a higher rate than main homes and to ensure that
people on low incomes are protected from unaffordable
charges. Replacing council tax with a proportional property
tax could also boost housing supply, some argue by hundreds
of thousands of homes (Lewis 2021).

Better taxation is not enough to fix our housing market of
course, or to ensure that people struggling on low incomes can
have a home which is safe, stable and affordable. We also need to:

1.   Build more social housing. Independent analysis of the
need for different kinds of homes has found that we need
145,000 more social homes per year; last year we built just
7 per cent of what is required. The government's current
Affordable Homes Programme is set to deliver just 75,000 over
five years: about 375,000 short of what is needed (Earwaker
& Baxter 2020).

2.   Reform Right to Buy so that local authorities can keep
all of the proceeds of sales (at the moment the Treasury gets
most of them), can use the money to cover up to half of the
cost of new social homes (right now they're only allowed to
cover 30 per cent) and can top up that funding with other
money.

3.   Regulate the private rented sector more effectively. The
government has promised action in a Renters' Reform Bill
in 2022, but it is still unclear what this will cover. As the

Renters' Reform Coalition has said, as well as removing the right of landlords to evict people without a reason, it should also introduce indefinite tenancies and create a register of landlords.

We should also create better routes to affordable home ownership for people on low to middle incomes, both to ease pressure on the private rented sector and because it is a dream for enormous numbers of people at all income levels. The only policy that has ever helped large numbers of people on low incomes to buy their homes was Right to Buy. In its first decade, an average of 100,000 people a year bought their homes (DCLG 2015). After that, however, the failure to replace the sold homes turned one of the biggest public policy successes into a massive failure. That failure cut off the path to home ownership for those on low incomes and drove up poverty and homelessness. Many low-income renters feel closer to homelessness than home ownership. Building social housing and reforming Right to Buy could be complemented by policies such as the Centre for Policy Studies' suggestion of creating long-term low-interest mortgages for first-time buyers (Edwards 2015), increasing overall housebuilding and creating incentives for small buy-to-let landlords to sell up and exit the market.

TAXING EARNINGS

The way we tax income from work varies depending on whether someone is an employee or works for themselves by being self-employed or working for their own company. The latter are taxed much more lightly than employees. That is unfair and inefficient. It's also increasingly significant as self-employment has grown much faster than employment in recent years.

The structure of the tax system has encouraged two phenomena. First, the growth in people choosing to work as self-employed or for their own companies instead of becoming employees, to reduce their tax. That is problematic because it reduces tax revenues and is unfair on those who can't make that choice. Second, "bogus self-employment" where people are pressured to work as self-employed because their employer wants to reduce the cost of workers in terms of tax and denying them rights such as sick pay, holiday pay, pension contributions and protection from unfair treatment. This creates insecurity, worse conditions and lower pay for workers, and it distorts and reduces the tax take which pays for public services.

The historical justification given for self-employed people paying less tax is often that they have lower entitlement to benefits. However, as the Institute for Government concludes: "There is no clear economic rationale for this different tax treatment ... in practice the difference between the rights that employees and the self-employed accrue are far too small to justify the different tax treatment" (Tetlow & Marshall 2019). Governments have been wary of equalizing the tax treatment of self-employed people with employees. It was last tried in 2017 when the chancellor, Philip Hammond, tried to increase the national insurance contributions paid by self-employed people to narrow the gap with those paid by employees. However, he was quickly forced to backtrack after Conservative MPs threatened to rebel. The economic rationale for the national insurance change was clear, and its impact was progressive: most low-earning self-employed people would either see no change or would actually pay less tax, whereas the losses were mainly among the relatively small group earning more than £47,000 a year. As the Resolution Foundation set out, "the majority of revenue raised will be from the richest tenth of households, while almost none comes from the bottom half" (Tomlinson 2017). In 2017, reality lost against a persistent media narrative and internal Conservative Party conflict. It is high time another government tried again.

TAXING GLOBAL CORPORATIONS

We have already seen that global corporations, particularly the tech giants, have leapt ahead of our current approach to regulating markets to protect consumers. The same is true of our tax system. Our taxes are designed for companies that are "resident" in the UK, on the principle that profits should be taxed in the country where they are made. Multinational companies, however, have become extremely adept at structuring themselves to minimize their tax exposure. This has led to international competition to reduce corporate tax rates in order to attract investment.

Between 2000 and 2018, the average corporate tax rate in the OECD fell from 32.2 per cent to 23.7 per cent. Although the average revenue from corporate taxes rose slightly from 2.6 per cent of GDP in 1996 to 2.9 per cent in 2016, it would have been far higher if it had kept pace with the growth in wealth creation by businesses. The Institute for Government argues that digital companies are especially hard to tax, for two reasons, one conceptual and the other practical. Conceptually, digital companies make most of their money from advertising and gathering user data, and they often deliver services without any physical presence in the consumer's country. In many cases it's unclear which government should be able to tax them. Practically, it is hard for a government to collect VAT on high numbers of small transactions, with goods bought through digital platforms, from foreign suppliers.

In recent years a consensus has grown that the only way to get a grip on this is with international cooperation. In May 2019, the OECD and G20 countries agreed to work on a joint solution. In 2021, 130 countries agreed to set a new minimum tax rate for corporate income (OECD 2021). The rate was set at 15 per cent and should come into force in 2023. The new system will also direct some of the taxes of large multinational companies to the countries where their products or services are sold, instead of only being collected by the country where they have set up their headquarters. The OECD estimates that multinational companies have managed to sidestep paying somewhere between $100 billion and $240 billion of taxes a year by exploiting the "gaps and mismatches between different countries' tax systems" (Dangor 2021). This agreement does not present a full solution, but it was a significant milestone in creating a new international approach to taxing global companies, which can and should be built on.

Conclusion

Poverty is fundamentally about power and powerlessness. The workers with the least power can't avoid jobs that trap them in poverty. The least valuable consumers can't get the best prices. Those without economic and social power are held back, ground down and exposed to public services that treat them at best as children or at worst as cogs in the machine. They don't have the economic power to avoid the social security system or buy better mental health treatment. They don't have the social power to assert their rights or persuade providers to behave with compassion. They don't have the political power to challenge stereotypes or change the direction of policy.

Prejudice and discrimination strip away another layer of power, leaving disabled people, some Black and minority ethnic groups and women with even fewer options and less leverage to change their situation.

When Beveridge proposed the industrial welfare state he did so in an age when the industrial working classes were claiming more power through organized labour. But he and his ilk were still the products of the age of deference and the structures and systems he designed reflect that. His five giants still stalk the UK, but to defeat their modern incarnations we need a new rebalancing of power for a new technological age.

We have to rebalance digital markets to empower consumers;

rebalance labour markets so they offer better jobs and careers paths for workers; rebalance the housing market to create stable homes; rebalance our tax system to tap into wealth and revive fairness; and rebalance our public services to put users in the driving seat and relationships at their heart.

We can't defeat the giants of Want, Disease, Ignorance, Squalor and Idleness by shuffling a bit of money around or tweaking a few policies. We need to rethink what kind of society we want to live in, using the post-pandemic moment to remake those parts of our economy and our state that are no longer fit for purpose. This time around it won't be good enough for us to hand down solutions from on high and expect the grateful masses to queue up to buy them as they did in 1942. Nor can the changes that we need to make be done by stealth. They need to emerge from public deliberation and have the backing of democratic consent.

To gain that consent, we need a grown-up public debate about our collective goals and expectations. The Brexit referendum campaign was a missed opportunity for this (whether you agree with the result or not). It should have been a time for a real public conversation about what kind of country we aspire to become and what our place in the world should be. Instead, debate was dominated by people denying the clear trade-offs that should have been at the heart of the decision. Remainers often seemed to deny that being part of the EU involved any loss of sovereignty or national control, whereas many Leavers argued that there would be no economic penalty for leaving a huge trading bloc and its free market. What we didn't debate was what degree of national autonomy we felt it was reasonable to give up in return for the economic benefits of membership and protection of being part of a big club in a dangerous world. Ironically, the only person I really remember being honest about this was Nigel Farage, during one hostile interview in which he admitted that he was willing to accept some economic damage in return for greater national control. Whether you agree or disagree, that's a reasonable position and it shouldn't have been something that occasionally slipped out. Similarly, Remainers should have been honest about their view that they were willing to cede some national sovereignty in return for the benefits of being part of the EU.

Very little airtime was spent working through the options to keep the peace in Northern Ireland if we left. Or what kind of food system we want to have and how to balance costs for consumers, environmental concerns, farmers' livelihoods and safe supply chains. Or how to create opportunities and raise living standards for those people and places in the UK which had long been shut out of prosperity and were disenchanted with the workings of the global economy. As so often happens, the Punch and Judy show of politics swamped any chance of a mature public debate.

I have offered some ideas in this book of how we can slay the giant of Want and free people from poverty. But perhaps the most important message is that the industrial age is over, and the days of "social reformers know best" are gone. We must lean in to a digital, democratic, low-carbon future. To succeed we have to engage the public in creating solutions to modern-day social evils. That must start with an explicit and deliberate conversation about what a modern welfare state should aim to achieve and an honest examination of the trade-offs and choices involved in creating it. Only with this basis can we build something that will be fit for the next 80 years.

References

Abey, J. & A. Harrop 2021. *Going with the Grain: How to Increase Social Security with Public Support.* London: Fabian Society.

Aitken, A., P. Dolton & R. Riley 2018. *The Impact of the National Living Wage on Employment, Hours and Wages.* London: Low Pay Commission.

Altman, R. 2020. "What will the current crisis do to the state pension triple lock?" *Pension and Savings.* https://pensionsandsavings.com/what-will-current-crisis-do-to-the-state-pension-triple-lock/.

Apps, P. 2015. "Right to buy to let". *Inside Housing*, 14 August.

Banks, N. *et al.* 2014. *Climate Change and Social Justice: An Evidence Review.* York: Joseph Rowntree Foundation.

Barnard, H. 2018. *UK Poverty 2018.* York: Joseph Rowntree Foundation.

Baumberg, B. *et al.* 2012. *Benefits Stigma in Britain.* London: Turn2us.

Bell, T. 2019. "Doubling down on a bigger state: assessing labour's 2019 manifesto". London: Resolution Foundation.

Borkin, S. 2019. "Platform co-operatives: solving the capital conundrum". London: Nesta.

Bourquin, P. *et al.* 2019. "Living standards, poverty and inequality in the UK: 2019". London: Institute for Fiscal Studies.

Bourquin, P. & T. Waters 2019. "The tax system reduces inequality – but benefits do most of the heavy lifting". London: Institute for Fiscal Studies.

Brander, P. *et al.* 2020. *COMPASS Manual for Human Rights Education with Young People.* Council of Europe. https://rm.coe.int/compass-eng-rev-2020-web/1680a08e40.

Bray, R. *et al.* 2019. "The hidden dimensions of poverty". International Movement ATD Fourth World, Pierrelaye. https://www.atd-

fourthworld.org/wp-content/uploads/sites/5/2019/05/Dim_
Pauvr_eng_FINAL_July.pdf.

Brien, P. & M. Keep 2018. "The public finances: a historical overview".
Research briefing. House of Commons Library.

Brocek, F. 2019. "Is the link between productivity and wage growth
still alive in the UK?" Briefing, University of Strathclyde,
Fraser of Allandar Institute. https://fraserofallander.org/
link-labour-productivity-wage-growth-uk/.

Brook, P. 2018. "Life on a housing treadmill: struggling to make a
home on a low income". Joseph Rowntree Foundation.
https://www.jrf.org.uk/blog/life-housing-treadmill-struggling-
make-home-low-income.

Brook, P. 2021. "How to make jobs work and end the injustice of
working in poverty". York: Joseph Rowntree Foundation.

Burke, J. *et al.* 2020. "Distributional impacts of a carbon tax in the UK".
Policy brief, March. LSE Grantham Institute.

Business, Innovation and Skills Committee 2016. "Employment
practices at Sports Direct". Committee Session Report, House
of Commons. https://publications.parliament.uk/pa/cm201617/
cmselect/cmbis/219/219.pdf.

Butler, P. 2015. "Tenants hit by bedroom tax suffer range of health
problems, study shows". *The Guardian*, 16 March.

Butler, P. 2018. "Ban on housing benefit for 18 to 21 year-olds scrapped".
The Guardian, 29 March. https://www.theguardian.com/society/
2018/mar/29/ban-on-housing-benefit-for-18-to-21-year-olds-
scrapped.

Centre for Social Justice 2020. "Commissioning excellence in disability:
an assessment of the department for work and pensions national
contracted disability employment provision". London: Centre for
Social Justice.

Chase, E. & G. Bantebya-Kyomuhendo (eds) 2014. *Poverty and Shame:
Global Experiences*. Oxford: Oxford University Press.

Citizens Advice 2015. "Bogus self-employment costing millions to
workers and government". Press release, 19 August.

Clarke, S. 2019. "Coming of age during a downturn can cause scarring,
and it takes up to a decade to heal". London: Resolution Foundation.

Coleman, L., M. Dali-Chaouch and C. Harding 2020. "Childcare
survey 2020". Coram Family and Childcare. https://www.
familyandchildcaretrust.org/childcare-survey-2020.

Competition and Markets Authority 2021. "Algorithms: how they
can reduce competition and harm consumers". 19 January.
London: CMA.

Co-operatives UK. 2021. *The Co-op Economy Report 2021*. Manchester: Co-operatives UK.

Corlett, A. 2018. "Passing on: options for reforming inheritance taxation". London: Resolution Foundation.

Costa Dias, M., R. Joyce & F. Parodi 2018. "Wage progression and the gender wage gap: the causal impact of hours of work". London: Institute for Fiscal Studies.

Cottam, H. 2018. *Radical Help: How We Can Remake the Relationships between Us and Revolutionise the Welfare State*. London: Virago.

Cottam, H. 2020. "Welfare 5.0: why we need a social revolution and how to make it happen". UCL Institute for Innovation and Public Purpose.

Cottam, H. 2021. "The radical way: shifting the social paradigm". 13 May. https://www.hilarycottam.com/the-radical-way_shifting-the-social-paradigm/.

Coughlan, S. 2018. "Water bill 'too expensive' to flush toilet". *BBC News*. https://www.bbc.co.uk/news/education-46431480.

Dangor, G. 2021. "G20 signs off on 15% global minimum corporate tax – here's how it will work". *Forbes*.

Datta, N., G. Giupponi & S. Machin 2019. "Zero-hours contracts and labour market policy". *Economic Policy* 34(99): 369–427.

Denys, N. *et al.* 2018. "New blue: ideas for a new generation". London: Centre for Policy Studies.

Department for Business, Energy and Industrial Strategy 2020. "Trade union membership, UK 1995–2019: statistical bulletin". London: DBEIS.

Department for Communities and Local Government (DCLG) 2015. "Live table 678: annual social housing sales for England". London: DCLG.

Department for Education 2018. "Childcare and early years survey of parents 2018". London: Department for Education.

Department for Work and Pensions 2014. "Evaluation of the removal of the Spare Room Subsidy". London: DWP.

Department for Work and Pensions 2018. "Disability Confident Scheme: summary findings from a survey of participating employers". London: DWP.

Disability Benefits Consortium 2019. "Has welfare become unfair?"

Dixon, S., C. Smith & A. Touchet 2018. "The disability perception gap". London: Scope.

Dromey, J., L. Dewar & J. Finnegan 2020. "Tackling single parent poverty after coronavirus". London: Learning and Work Institute.

Dudding, A. 2021. "We must loosen poverty's grip on black,

Asian and ethnic minority people". York: Joseph Rowntree Foundation.

Earwaker, R. & D. Baxter 2020. "Build, build, build social housing: to stimulate our economy and unlock people from poverty and homelessness". York: Joseph Rowntree Foundation.

Earwaker, R. & J. Eliott 2021. "Renters on low incomes face a policy black hole: homes for social rent are the answer". York: Joseph Rowntree Foundation.

Education Endowment Foundation 2021. "Best evidence on impact of Covid-19 on pupil attainment". London: Education Endowment Foundation.

Edwards, G. 2015. "Resentful renters: how Britain's housing market went wrong and how to fix it". London: Centre for Policy Studies.

Elliott, I. 2016. "Poverty and mental health: a review to inform the Joseph Rowntree Foundation's anti-poverty strategy". Mental Health Foundation. https://www.mentalhealth.org.uk/sites/ default/files/Poverty%20and%20Mental%20Health.pdf.

Equality and Human Rights Commission 2015. "'Is Britain fairer'? Key facts and findings on young people".

Fair By Design 2021. "The poverty premium". London: Barrow Cadbury Trust.

Ferrari, E. *et al.* 2018. "Families in the North/Glasgow locked out of jobs market by 'unaffordable and unreliable' local transport". York: Joseph Rowntree Foundation.

Fitzpatrick, S. *et al.* 2016. "Destitution in UK". York: Joseph Rowntree Foundation.

Freud, D. 2021. *Clashing Agendas: Inside the Welfare Trap.* London: Nine Elms.

Gangham, G. 2019. "Game of homes: the rise of multiple property ownership in Great Britain". London: Resolution Foundation.

Gardiner, L. 2019. "The shifting shape of social security". London: Resolution Foundation.

Gardiner, L. *et al.* 2020. "An intergenerational audit for the UK". London: Resolution Foundation.

Garthwaite, K. 2016. "Stigma, shame and 'people like us': an ethnographic study of foodbank use in the UK". *Journal of Poverty and Social Justice* 24(3): 277–89.

Gingerbread 2020. *Caring without Sharing: Single Parents' Journey through the Covid-19 Crisis – Interim Report.* London: Gingerbread.

Goulden, C. 2010. "Cycles of poverty, unemployment and low pay". York: Joseph Rowntree Foundation.

Gousy, H. 2014. "Can't complain: why poor conditions prevail in private

rented homes". Policy report. Shelter. https://england.shelter.org.
uk/__data/assets/pdf_file/0006/892482/6430_04_9_Million_
Renters_Policy_Report_Proof_10_opt.pdf.

Hawking, M. 2019. "How local industrial strategies can deliver inclusive growth". York: Joseph Rowntree Foundation.

Henehan, K. 2021. "Uneven steps: changes in youth unemployment and study since the onset of Covid-19". London: Resolution Foundation.

Hewitt, B. 2021. "Collapsed ceilings, mice and mould: appalling conditions uncovered on housing estate of 500 homes". *ITV News*. https://www.itv.com/news/2021-06-16/collapsed-ceilings-mice-and-mould-appalling-conditions-uncovered-across-an-entire-housing-estate-of-nearly-500-homes.

Hirsch, D. *et al.* 2015. "How much is enough? Reaching social consensus on minimum household needs". Loughborough University. https://www.lboro.ac.uk/media/wwwlboroacuk/content/crsp/downloads/reports/How%20much%20is%20enough.pdf.

Hirsch, D. *et al.* 2018. "A minimum income standard for the UK 2008–2018: continuity and change". York: Joseph Rowntree Foundation.

Home Affairs Committee 2018. "Immigration policy: basis for building consensus, 15 January 2018, HC 500 of session 2017–19". London: House of Commons.

Hood, A. & T. Waters 2017. "The impact of tax and benefit changes on household incomes". London: Institute for Fiscal Studies.

Howard, M. 2018. "Universal credit and financial abuse: exploring the links". London: Women's Budget Group.

Independent Age 2020. "Credit where it's due: a briefing on low uptake of pension credit". London: Independent Age.

Independent Chief Inspector of Borders and Immigration 2007. *An Inspection of the Right to Rent Scheme*. London: HMSO.

Inglis, G. *et al.* 2019. "Health inequality implications from a qualitative study of experiences of poverty stigma in Scotland". *Social Science & Medicine* 232(July): 43–9.

Ingold, D. & S. Soper 2016. "Amazon doesn't consider the race of its customers: should it?". *Bloomberg*. https://www.bloomberg.com/graphics/2016-amazon-same-day/.

Innes, D. 2018. "The links between low productivity and in-work poverty". York: Joseph Rowntree Foundation.

Innes, D. 2020. "What has driven the rise of in-work poverty?" York: Joseph Rowntree Foundation.

John, E., G. Thomas & A. Touchet 2019. "The disability price tag 2019". London: Scope.

Joint Council for the Welfare of Immigrants 2016. "Submission of evidence re. SI 2016 No.11 (C.2): Immigration Act 2014 (Commencement No.6) Order 2016". London: UK Parliament.

Joseph Rowntree Foundation 2016. *UK Poverty: Causes, Costs and Solutions*. York: Joseph Rowntree Foundation.

Joseph Rowntree Foundation 2021. "Is universal basic income a good idea?" https://www.jrf.org.uk/report/universal-basic-income-good-idea.

Katwala, S. 2021. "Britain's racism problem – we've made progress, but not enough". *Prospect*, 14 July.

Kelley, N. & R. Wishart 2019. "Attitudes of people on a low income: work". York: Joseph Rowntree Foundation.

Kelly, G. & D. Tomlinson 2018. "Putting tech to work: the urgent need for innovation in how the low-wage workforce is supported". Resolution Trust. http://resolutiontrust.org/wp-content/uploads/2016/11/Putting-tech-to-work.pdf.

Khan, O. 2020. "The colour of money". London: Runnymede Trust.

Kotecha, M., S. Arthur & S. Coutinho 2013. "Understanding the relationship between pensioner poverty and material deprivation". Research Report 827. Sheffield: Department for Work and Pensions.

Learning and Work Institute 2019. *Evidence Review: Employment Support for People with Disabilities and Health Conditions*. Learning and Work Institute. https://learningandwork.org.uk/resources/research-and-reports/evidence-review-employment-support-for-people-with-disabilities-and-health-conditions/.

Lent, A. & J. Studdert 2021. "The community paradigm: why public services need radical change and how it can be achieved". London: New Local.

Leonard Cheshire 2019. "Reimaging the workplace: disability and inclusive employment". London: Leonard Cheshire.

Leslie, J. & K. Shah 2021. "(Wealth) gap year". London: Resolution Foundation.

Leslie, J. 2020. "The missing billions". London: Resolution Foundation.

Lewis, C. 2021. "Property news from the 2021 Conservative Party conference". *The Times*, 8 October.

Li, Y. & A. Heath 2018. "Persisting disadvantages: a study of labour market dynamics of ethnic unemployment and earnings in the UK (2009–2015)". *Journal of Ethnic and Migration Studies* 46(5): 857–78.

Lindsay, C. 2014. "Work first versus human capital development in employability programs". University of Strathclyde.

Lodge, T. 2020. "The great carbon swindle". London: Centre for Policy Studies.

Low Pay Commission 2020. "Non-compliance and enforcement of the National Minimum Wage". London: Low Pay Commission.

Lynn, G. & E. Davey 2013. "London letting agents 'refuse black tenants'". *BBC News*, 14 October.

Mackey, A. & R. McInnes 2020. "Contributory benefits and social insurance in the UK". London: House of Commons Library.

Manji, A. 2020. "People, not tick-boxes: a call to rebuild the disability benefits system". London: Mind.

Mayer, C. 2020. "It's time to redefine the purpose of business: here's a roadmap". World Economic Forum. https://www.weforum.org/agenda/2020/01/its-time-for-a-radical-rethink-of-corporate-purpose/.

McCormick, J. & D. Hay 2020. *Poverty in Scotland 2020.* York: Joseph Rowntree Foundation.

McDonald, R. & A. Sandor 2020. "Making work secure: unlocking poverty and building a stronger economy". York: Joseph Rowntree Foundation.

McKee, R. 2018. "The Citizens' Assembly behind the Irish Abortion Referendum". London: Involve.

Moffatt, S. *et al.* 2015. "A qualitative study of the impact of the UK 'bedroom tax'". *Journal of Public Health* 38(2) 197–205.

Moran, C. 2012. "Why I love the welfare state". *The Times.* https://www.thetimes.co.uk/article/why-i-love-the-welfare-state-zmd25qbvtkq.

Nuffield Trust 2020. "Supporting patients to manage their long-term conditions". London: Nuffield Trust.

Nwaobasi, C. 2020. "A personal history of experiencing racism in the UK". Virgin Limited Edition, 30 October.

Oakley, M. 2021. "Time to think again: disability benefits and support after Covid-19". London: Social Market Foundation.

OECD 2014. "The crisis and its aftermath: a stress test for societies and for social policies". In *Society at a Glance 2014.* Paris: OECD.

OECD 2020. *Revenue Statistics 2020: The United Kingdom.* Paris: OECD.

OECD 2021. "130 countries and jurisdictions join bold new framework for international tax reform". Press release.

Office for Budget Responsibility 2015. *Welfare Trends Report.* London: OBR.

Office for Budget Responsibility 2021. *Overview of the October 2021 Economic and Fiscal Outlook.* London: OBR.

Office for National Statistics 2016. "Women shoulder the responsibility of unpaid work". London: ONS.

Office for National Statistics 2019. "Which occupations are at highest risk of being automated?" London: ONS.

Office for National Statistics 2020. "Domestic abuse victim characteristics: England and Wales – year ending March 2020". London: ONS.

Office for Tax Simplification 2020. "OTS capital gains tax review: simplifying by design". London: Office for Tax Simplification.

Ortiz-Ospina, E. 2017. "Historical poverty reductions: more than a story about 'free-market capitalism'". *Our World in Data*, 29 September.

Parveen, N. & T. Thomas 2021. "I was terrified: pupils tell of being victimised in UK schools". *The Guardian*, 24 March.

Plunkett, J. 2021. *End State: 9 Ways Society Is Broken and How We fix It*. London: Trapeze.

Poverty and Social Exclusion 2013. *Breadline Britain: 1983–2013 – UK Life Stories*. Poverty and Social Exclusion. https://www.poverty.ac.uk/living-poverty/breadline-britain-1983-2013.

Richardson, J. 2021. "The insecurity complex: low paid workers and the growth of insecure work". London: Living Wage Foundation.

Rogaly, K., J. Elliott & D. Baxter 2021. "What's causing structural racism in housing?" York: Joseph Rowntree Foundation.

Runnymede Trust 2013. "'No Dogs, No Blacks' new findings show that minority ethnic groups are still discriminated against when trying to rent private housing". London: The Runnymede Trust.

Ryan, F. 2019. *Crippled: Austerity and the Demonization of Disabled People*. London: Verso.

Sayce, L. 2011. "Getting in, staying in and getting on disability employment support fit for the future". London: Department for Work and Pensions.

Schmuecker, K. *et al.* 2021. "Making jobs work: improvements to job quality are key to our recovery". York: Joseph Rowntree Foundation.

Seaman, E. *et al.* 2020. "In focus: experiences of older age in England". London: Independent Age.

Sehmi, R. 2021 "Out of the woods? Young people's mental health and labour market status as the economy reopens". London: Resolution Foundation.

Shildrick, T. 2018. "Lessons from Grenfell: poverty propaganda, stigma and class power". *Sociological Review* 66(4): 783–98.

Smith, A. 1776. *An Inquiry into Nature and Causes of the Wealth of Nations*.

Social Metrics Commission 2018. "A new measure of poverty for the UK". London: Social Metrics Commission.

Social Mobility Commission 2020. "Monitoring social mobility 2013–2020: is the government delivering on our recommendations?" London: Social Metrics Commission.

Social Security Advisory Committee 2020. "How DWP involves disabled people when developing or evaluating programmes that affect them". London: Social Security Advisory Committee.

Social Security Advisory Committee 2021. "Jobs and benefits: the COVID-19 challenge". London: Social Security Advisory Committee.

Stasio, V. & A. Heath 2019. "Are employers in Britain discriminating against ethnic minorities?" Nuffield College, Oxford. http://csi.nuff.ox.ac.uk/wp-content/uploads/2019/01/Are-employers-in-Britain-discriminating-against-ethnic-minorities_final.pdf.

Takala, H. 2020. "Access to Work is a policy success – but more people should be able to benefit from it". London: Institute for Employment Studies.

Taylor, M. 2016. *Good Work: The Taylor Review of Modern Working Practices*. London: Department for Business, Energy and Industrial Strategy.

Tetlow, G. & J. Marshall 2019. "Taxing times: the need to reform the UK tax system". London: Institute for Government.

Timpson, J. 2019. "Call it cobblers but we believe in making our people happy". *Sunday Times*, 25 August.

Tomlinson, D. 2017. "A small and sensible National Insurance rise for the self-employed is not the real strivers tax". London: Resolution Foundation.

Townsend, P. 1979. *Poverty in the United Kingdom*. London: Penguin.

Trades Union Congress (TUC) 2020. "Forced out: the cost of getting childcare wrong". London: Trades Union Congress.

Trades Union Congress (TUC) 2021. "TUC action plan to reform labour market enforcement". London: Trades Union Congress.

Turner Lee, N., P. Resnick & G. Barton 2019. "Algorithmic bias detections and mitigation: best practices and policies to reduce consumer harms". Washington, DC: Brookings Institution.

United Nations 2001. *Poverty and the International Covenant on Economic, Social and Cultural Rights*. New York: United Nations.

Van Ham, D. & M. David 2012. "Segregation, choice based letting and social housing: how housing policy can affect the segregation process". IZA Discussion Papers, No. 6372. Institute for the Study of Labour, Bonn.

Walby, S. & J. Allen 2004. "Domestic violence, sexual assault and stalking: findings from the British Crime Survey". London: Home Office.

Wenham, A. & A. Sandor 2021. "People in low paid, insecure work faced a rising tide of employment uncertainty in 2020". York: Joseph Rowntree Foundation.

Willetts, D. 2018. "Baby boomers are going to have to pay more tax on their wealth to fund health and social care". London: Resolution Foundation.

Women's Budget Group 2018. "The female face of poverty". London: Women's Budget Group.

Wood, M. *et al.* 2009. "A test for racial discrimination in recruitment practice in British cities". London: Department for Work and Pensions.

Work and Pensions Committee 2019. "The benefit cap". UK Parliament.

Work and Pensions Select Committee 2018. "PIP and ESA Assessments". London: UK Parliament.

Yaqoob, T. & I. Shahnaz 2021. "Freeing low-income single parents from in-work poverty's grip". York: Joseph Rowntree Foundation.

Young, S. 2021. "How social security can deliver for disabled people in Scotland". York: Joseph Rowntree Foundation.

Young Women's Trust 2020. "Young women facing constant financial struggle". London: Young Women's Trust.

Index

Note: Page numbers in *italic* refer to figures